King Alfred

Twayne's English Authors Series

George D. Economou, Editor

University of Oklahoma

TEAS 425

King Alfred

By Allen J. Frantzen

Loyola University of Chicago

Twayne Publishers
A Division of G.K. Hall & Co. • Boston

Copyright © 1986 by G.K. Hall & Co.
All Rights Reserved
Published by Twayne Publishers
A Division of G.K. Hall & Co.
70 Lincoln Street
Boston, Massachusetts 02111

Book production by Elizabeth Todesco
Book design by Barbara Anderson

Typeset in 11 pt. Garamond
by P&M Typesetting, Inc., Waterbury, Connecticut

Printed on permanent/durable acid-free paper
and bound in the United States of America

Library of Congress Cataloging-in-Publication Data

Frantzen, Allen J.
  King Alfred.

  (Twayne's English authors series; TEAS 425)
  Bibliography: p. 136
  Includes index.
    1. Alfred, King of England, 849–899—Criticism and
interpretation.   2. Anglo-Saxon prose literature—
Translations from Latin—History and criticism.
3. Latin prose literature—Translations into Anglo-Saxon
—History and criticism.   4. Latin language—Translating
into Anglo-Saxon.   I. Title.   II. Series.
PR1564.F73   1986   829'.8   85-27310
ISBN 0-8057-6918-8

To the memory of my mother

Contents

About the Author

Allen J. Frantzen is an Associate Professor of English at Loyola University of Chicago and formerly taught at Oberlin College. He received his B.A. from Loras College, Dubuque, Iowa, and his M.A. and Ph.D. from the University of Virginia. His publications include *The Literature of Penance in Anglo-Saxon England* (Rutgers University Press, 1983) and numerous articles about medieval literature and literary history in *Speculum, Anglo-Saxon England*, the *Journal of Ecclesiastical History*, the *Review of English Studies*, the *Chaucer Review*, and other journals.

Preface

As the major figure of Anglo-Saxon literature in the ninth century, King Alfred has special claims on the student's attention. He was both an author and a statesman whose political achievements created a climate in which his literary endeavors could flourish. Among the kings and queens of England, others have been more learned, but none acquired learning in the face of graver threats to the kingdom's survival, more ardently pursued literature both as avocation and as policy, or achieved comparable literary eminence. Alfred is often called the Father of English prose, an epithet which overstates his achievement but justly testifies to his stature as the first major author in the history of vernacular prose. With the assistance of trained scholars, he translated four major Latin texts into English: The *Regula Pastoralis* of Gregory the Great, the *De Consolatione Philosophiae* of Boethius, the *Soliloquia* of Augustine, and the first fifty psalms from the Book of Psalms. In addition, Alfred compiled a law code, the first issued in England in one hundred years.

This study introduces the student to Alfred's place in Anglo-Saxon literary history and explains his program to revive learning in England after the devastating Viking invasions of the ninth century. Each of his translations is made the subject of a separate chapter which summarizes the text, reviews its manuscript tradition, examines its relationship to its Latin source, and comments on major critical issues. The objectives are to acquaint the student with Alfred's work and its sources, to explicate the texts and their critical traditions, and to encourage independent research. Familiarity with Alfred's translations is not assumed; all Latin and Old English passages are translated.

I wish to thank those who contributed their time and expertise to this project, especially Richard Clement and Patrick O'Neill for reading and commenting on several chapters, and Paul Szarmach and Ruth Waterhouse for offering advice and information. My students at Loyola University of Chicago—Daniel Driscoll, Mary Filkins, Joan Kaufman-Mullin, Mary Murphy, Rebecca Thomas-Wilson, and Nancy Workman, members of a graduate seminar in Alfred's prose—

helped to shape my analysis of several texts discussed here. Elizabeth El Itreby Searles and James B. Denigan, Jr., read the typescript with care and contributed much to its improvement.

Extracts from *Alfred the Great: Asser's "Life of King Alfred" and Other Contemporary Sources,* translated by Simon Keynes and Michael Lapidge, © 1983 by Simon Keynes and Michael Lapidge, are reprinted by permission of Penguin Books Ltd.

I owe a special debt of gratitude to the Alexander von Humboldt Foundation, Bonn, West Germany, for research support; to Dr. and Mrs. Gerd Wollburg, for hospitality during my visits to Germany; and to George R. Paterson, for good counsel and expert criticism, generously given.

Allen J. Frantzen

Loyola University of Chicago

Chronology

Chapter One
King Alfred and His England
Alfred as an English Author

Alfred, King of Wessex, is the preeminent figure of English literature in the ninth century. He is remembered today not only for translating important Latin texts, but for defeating the Viking invaders and forging political alliances which led to the foundation of the English state. Perhaps no other English author has secured his place in history as much through his military and diplomatic achievements as through his literary merits. So important was his contribution to English literature that he would have won literary fame even had he not already been venerated as a monarch; but so important was his role in the formation of a united English kingdom that he would have been remembered for all ages even had he never written a word. Often called the Father of English prose, Alfred is also the only English monarch to be known as "the Great." He towers above other figures of the Anglo-Saxon period because he succeeded in inaugurating a national literature while shaping and defending a nation. "His unique importance in the history of English letters," wrote F. M. Stenton, "comes from his conviction that a life without knowledge or reflection was unworthy of respect, and his determination to bring the thought of the past within the range of his subjects' understanding. The translations of ancient books by which he tried to reach this end form the beginning of English prose literature."[1]

However, Alfred must be considered an author in a special sense. Like most writers of his day, he may not have penned his own works. Instead, he probably dictated them to professional scribes responsible for producing fair copies for publication. In addition to the assistance of scribes, Alfred depended heavily on the learning of scholars, several of whom he brought together to serve as his teachers. He frequently acknowledged their help, but it is difficult to know where Alfred's ideas ended and their ideas began. Thus, the literary works attributed to him are best regarded as a collective achievement supervised by Alfred and guided by his spirit.

Because we cannot determine precisely what he did or did not write, Alfred's reputation for learning inevitably rests on a layer of myth.[2] According to Asser, his contemporary and biographer, and hence our chief source for information about the king, Alfred began to read and translate Latin with extraordinary ease—in a single day, an accomplishment we may wish to regard with some suspicion.[3] However, no reservations about Alfred's role in the texts attributed to him have inhibited those determined to enshrine him in drama, epic poetry, and music—including opera—as England's holiest, wisest, and most valiant monarch.[4] Likewise, the titles found in scholarly bibliographies give equal weight to Alfred's learned and political achievements: for example, *The Millenary of Alfred the Great, Warrior and Saint, Scholar and King*,[5] or *Alfred the Great, the Truth Teller, Maker of England, 848–899*.[6] Some of this enthusiasm to praise Alfred sprang from the historical coincidence which in 1901 juxtaposed the millenary observance of his death with the demise of that other greatly revered monarch, Queen Victoria.[7] The eminent historian, Charles Plummer, fellow and chaplain of Corpus Christi College, Oxford, eulogized the two monarchs together:

Will not the historian of the future see a certain sad appropriateness in the fact that the Queen should have died in the year which is to celebrate the millenary of the death of this, the greatest of her ancestors, the one whom she so much resembled in her unswerving loyalty to duty, her constant labour for the good of her people, her unfaltering allegiance to truth?[8]

It is a measure of Plummer's patriotism, and his politics, that he stoutly defended Alfred against amateur historians, ever eager to find in Alfred signs of their own political enthusiasms. The king, insisted Plummer, was not "a nineteenth-century radical with a touch of the nonconformist conscience; or a Broad-Churchman with agnostic proclivities."[9] But neither Plummer's strictures nor the passing of the Victorian age extinguished the urge to romanticize the king. In 1969 the reading public was urged to explore Victor Hastings's "lusty novel," *Alfred the Great*, and to see the "sensational" motion picture on which it had been based.[10] Victorian admiration has occasionally reappeared both in scholarly dress—in Eleanor Shipley Duckett's old-fashioned but excellent 1956 biography, for example—and in somewhat more popular guise, in Alfred J. Mapp's vivid and imaginative 1974 rendering of Alfred's life.[11]

But modern scholars characteristically occupy themselves with more sober concerns, such as the language, dates, and sources of Alfred's translations, and their efforts have tempered admiration for Alfred's work. Leaders of the current critical reassessment, reluctant to eulogize the king's personal and moral greatness, seek to debunk many myths about him.[12] Observing this process, one commentator has remarked that "it may become fashionable to 'de-mythologize' Alfred by considering him neither the father of the English navy nor the father of English prose, but rather merely the father of Edward the Elder."[13] However, Alfred's accomplishments as statesman, philosopher, warrior, and man of letters cannot be dismissed as mere fabrications of patriotic adulation and literary mythmaking.

Alfred became known as "the Great" only in the sixteenth century.[14] But his legendary reputation owes its beginning to the *Life* by Asser, published shortly after Alfred's death, and to the works of the twelfth-century historian, William of Malmesbury.[15] Mythical and apocryphal elements frequently were incorporated into later sources. An example is the famous story of Alfred and the cakes, in which the king, in hiding as a refugee, acquires humility when he is scolded by a herdsman's wife for allowing her bread to burn.[16] Other myths about Alfred appear in two early Middle English poems, *The Proverbs of Alfred*[17] and *The Owl and the Nightingale*.[18] Thus, three centuries after his death Alfred had acquired a reputation as a wise man, if not yet as England's most learned monarch.

Sources contemporary with King Alfred provide a more reliable record of his accomplishments. In addition to Asser's *Life* and the commentary of William of Malmesbury, the early sources include treaties, laws, the king's own will, and the *Anglo-Saxon Chronicle* for the years 888–899 (possibly a product of Alfred's court).[19] The contemporary materials supplement and complement the picture presented by Alfred's own translations and must be read alongside his works. Not surprisingly, these sources create a coherent view of his achievement that would clearly have met with the approval of Alfred and his followers. For that very reason, some of them, the *Anglo-Saxon Chronicle* in particular, have sometimes been viewed as propaganda produced at Alfred's command. "Propaganda" has many meanings, of course, not all of them derogatory. To propagandize may mean to spread ideas and to indoctrinate, with or without distortion. We can readily understand why Alfred and his helpers wished to portray their achievements in the most favorable light possible.[20] Given

their access to literary means, they should be congratulated for understanding the power of literature not only to teach, but also to arouse
political loyalty. But the dispute about Alfred's possible manipulation
of history, however relevant to our assessment of his skill as a leader,
will play only a small role in the following pages. We will focus instead on the circumstances in which Alfred came to power and began
to write, and we will attempt to situate his translations in the fuller
context of ninth-century history.[21]

Alfred's Political and Historical Context

Alfred was born in 849 in Berkshire. He was the youngest of the
five sons of King Æthelwulf and a grandson of King Egbert, who
struggled for decades to extend the power of the West Saxon dynasty
into Mercia, Northumbria, Wales, and East Anglia.[22] During Egbert's reign (802–39) Viking incursions into England reached the
southern parts of the island. As Egbert checked the invaders' progress, he extended the boundaries of Wessex considerably to the east.
To help him govern these vast territories, Egbert appointed his son
Æthelwulf as King of Kent. Upon his succession to his father's
throne, Æthelwulf assigned the government of the eastern territories
to his eldest son, Alfred's brother, Æthelstan. When Æthelstan died
early in the 850s, Æthelwulf remained sole ruler of all the territories
conquered by Egbert.[23]

Alfred seems to have been removed from the struggle for power
that marked his father's reign. He was sent to Rome in 853, at age
four, and he returned there again two years later in the company of
his father, Æthelwulf. Before departing for Rome, Æthelwulf divided
the kingdom between two of Alfred's remaining elder brothers,
Æthelbald and Æthelberht. During Æthelwulf's absence, Æthelbald
schemed unsuccessfully to usurp his father's power. These schemes
were frustrated; it was only after Æthelbald's death in 860 that
Æthelberht achieved his ambition to rule the entire kingdom. Upon
his death in 865, the throne passed to Æthelred, the last of Alfred's
brothers, and Alfred was positioned as the heir apparent.

Alfred's ascent to power was not, therefore, easily accomplished.
The illusion that as a boy he was destined for greatness flourished
only in Alfred's later years, fed by stories of his early travels on the
Continent. In Rome Alfred had been made a consul and honored by
Pope Leo IV. The *Anglo-Saxon Chronicle* for 853 recounts this event as

a portent of greatness from Alfred's earliest years.[24] The claim that Alfred had been consecrated by the Pope, which is widely disputed, is possibly a reflection of a continental custom according to which future rulers were annointed in their youth.[25]

Æthelred died in 871, leaving Alfred to rule alone at a time when the Viking forces renewed their attacks in Wessex. They had arrived in England again in 865, had quartered in East Anglia, moved north, settled in Mercia, and soon thereafter attacked Wessex. During the period 865–878 Wessex alone retained its ruling dynasty, while other kingdoms in England were either overrun by the Vikings or taken over by puppet rulers under Viking control.[26] Not until 878, after a protracted struggle, did Alfred conclude a pact with the Viking king, Guthrum, in which the invaders agreed to withdraw entirely from Wessex. Alfred then repelled another Viking army from the Thames estuary. This force withdrew to the Continent in 880 and, until it returned in 892, Alfred ruled in relative peace.[27] During this time, temporarily freed from military crises, Alfred began his educational reforms and his translations.

Desiring education for himself and for his followers, and finding his kingdom poorly equipped with learned men to help him renew the kingdom's schools, Alfred sought trained assistants. Between 885 and 890 he appointed seven scholars as his helpers, four of them— Plegmund, Wærferth, Æthelstan, and Werwulf—from Mercia, where the learned tradition had remained relatively strong during the invasions. Two more were summoned from the Continent; these were John, from the eastern Frankish region, and Grimbald, one of Alfred's most important assistants, who came from St. Bertin's (a monastery in Flanders) after serving Archbishop Fulk in Reims.[28] Asser, Alfred's biographer, came from St. David's in Wales, and divided his time in 885–887 between Alfred's court and his home.

According to Alfred, the state of learning was severely depressed when he ascended the throne. In the preface to the *Pastoral Care* Alfred recalls the churches of his childhood as being filled with treasures and books, and "a great number of God's servants" who could not read them. The books were in Latin, and had not been translated into English because no one had ever imagined that Latin would cease to be widely used.[29] Alfred reported that he could find no learned men south of the Thames, and few priests to the north, in Mercia, or beyond that, north of the Humber River, who could translate Latin into English or even understand their service books.[30]

Historians frequently question this description of the state of learning, suspecting that the king's rhetoric is in some degree self-serving, and noting that it advances precisely the view of decline portrayed in the *Anglo-Saxon Chronicle* and related sources. Stenton claims that Alfred, writing in 894, "heavily overpainted the depression in English learning in 871."[31] R.H.C. Davis strongly criticizes the "misleading impression" created by the preface.[32] In a similar vein, D.P. Kirby argues that "it was the fact that men could read English books which gave Alfred the idea of rendering further important works in translation,"[33] and H.R. Loyn agrees that "there must have been some works in English in the early part of the ninth century."[34]

Taken at face value, Alfred's statements would mean that he found clergymen almost totally illiterate: if they could not read their Latin service manuals, they naturally could not translate them into their own language. Perhaps the king's description of the decline of learning is exaggerated. But we can understand his need to depict conditions in such a way that his efforts at renewal might seem more urgent and that others might be encouraged to join him. His preface to the *Pastoral Care*, along with Asser's *Life*, and the highly favorable account of Alfred found in the *Chronicle*, do more than praise the king. They also strive to excite enthusiasm for learning and literature in others. These sources portray Alfred's struggle to realize an ideal that must have seemed remote when he acceded to the throne—an England united under strong leadership and working to renew its learned tradition.

Alfred translated and encouraged translating not only because he hoped to create an educated clergy and nobility for the good of his nation, but also because he loved learning and literature. Alfred's preface to the *Dialogues* of Gregory the Great states that leaders such as himself needed to turn to "holy books" to "relax [their] minds in the midst of these earthly anxieties and turn them to the divine and spiritual law." As Dorothy Whitelock has noted, Alfred evidently requested a translation of the *Dialogues* "for his own use, and not expressly to increase the standard of learning in his kingdom."[35] He did not always require an audience other than himself for his translations.

This personal interest in literature balances the pragmatism usually seen in Alfred's educational reform. His translations frequently stress the idea that learning, because it improves the mind and the soul, makes life more rewarding and enjoyable. Books were important to Alfred even in his youth. Raised in a literary household, he is described by Asser as a boy listening attentively to English poems "day and night," and hearing them often recited by others, as well as memorizing them himself. But as an adult, Alfred must have found it difficult to turn his attention to the works of Gregory the Great, Augustine, or Boethius. Indeed, Asser remarks that Alfred lamented as the greatest "among all his difficulties and hindrances" in his adult life that,

at the time when he was of the right age and had the leisure and the capacity for learning, he did not have the teachers. For when he was older, and more incessantly preoccupied by day and night with—or rather harassed by—all kinds of illnesses unknown to the physicians of this island, as well as by the cares (both domestic and foreign) of the royal office, and also by the incursions of the Vikings by land and sea, he had the teachers and scribes to some small extent, but he was unable to study.[36]

Asser places so great a stress on Alfred's illnesses that some have speculated that the king's problems were in part psychological.[37] But the conflict between private concerns and public duties, and the competition between spiritual and secular affairs, seem to have marked all stages of Alfred's life. Comparatively little is known about the final years of his life. Because of the Vikings' return to England from the Continent, Alfred spent the last decade of his reign working to unify his kingdom in the face of renewed assault. According to William of Malmesbury, the king was translating the psalms at the time of his death, in 899. But while the surviving translation of this work appears without doubt to have been Alfred's, William's picture of Alfred laboring piously in his final days is not of certain accuracy. The defense of the kingdom preoccupied the king from first to last; the scholarship for which we revere him was never his principal concern.

Alfred's Canon

Scholars have not determined how much of the literature attributed to him Alfred himself wrote and how much was written by his assistants, the helpers mentioned in the preface to the *Pastoral Care* and in the preface to Wærferth's translation of Gregory's *Dialogues*. The preface to this latter work, written in the king's voice, is "spoken" by Alfred; in it, he claims that he "petitioned [his] true friends that they should write down for [him] from God's books the following teaching concerning the virtues and miracles of holy men."[38] In the preface to the *Pastoral Care* Alfred declares that his assistants helped him translate "certain books which [were] the most necessary for all men to know."[39]

The standard repertory of works attributed to Alfred was taken by early scholars from William of Malmesbury, who credited Alfred with the "greater part of Roman writings," including the *World History* of Orosius, Gregory's *Pastoral Care* and *Dialogues*, the *Consolation of Philosophy* by Boethius, the *Soliloquies* of Augustine, the *Ecclesiastical History* of Bede, the prose psalms of the *Paris Psalter*, a handbook of pious writings or *enchiridion*, and, finally, the *Anglo-Saxon Chronicle*.[40] But, as techniques for examining authorship have improved, the canon of works attributed to Alfred has steadily decreased; and, as records about his life have been scrutinized more carefully, some scholars have even questioned the extent of Alfred's role as "overseer" of the translations traditionally ascribed to him. While most of these works were probably produced during Alfred's reign, evidence of dialect and style has been used to reduce the canon of texts attributed to him to just five works: the translations of Augustine and Boethius, the *Pastoral Care*, the psalms, and a collection of laws.

In addition to translations he himself supervised, Alfred advanced the more general aims of his educational reform by requesting translations to be undertaken by others, and it is under this category that certain texts once attributed to Alfred should now be placed, including the *Dialogues* discussed above, which we know to have been translated at Alfred's request; Bede's *Ecclesiastical History*;[41] the Old English *Martyrology*;[42] the *World History* of Orosius;[43] and a book of medical lore or "leechbook."[44] Anyone wishing to appreciate the literary context of Alfred's England must study these texts. But because we know that Alfred did not translate them, and because we cannot be sure if most of them bear any certain relationship to his own literary program, they fall outside the limits of the present study.

Critical Caveats

Those reading Alfred's works for the first time should be made aware at the outset of certain critical problems, some of them not encountered in other Old English texts or in the literature of other periods. Three factors that complicate our analysis of his translations must be kept in mind when reading the chapters that follow. These are the concept of authorship; the Latin sources available to the king; and the sequence of Alfred's canon.

The first of these problems is our understanding of "authorship" as the term applies to King Alfred. His role in the texts attributed to him is difficult to distinguish from that of his helpers. They may have corrected his translations, suggested which texts to translate, and translated major portions of the texts themselves. Surely as he fought wars and supervised major building projects, designed ships and fortifications, and provided for an army, Alfred must have set aside his scholarly projects for months at a time. "Authorship" may therefore belong to the actual writer of a text, or to one who dictated the text to a scribe,[45] or simply to one who oversaw translations of Latin texts rather than produced them himself.

Our uncertainty about the authorship of some works once attributed to Alfred has given rise to various terms, altogether too nebulous, which scholars would do better to avoid. For example, texts excluded from Alfred's canon have been assigned to the "Alfredian circle." Of the figures from the "Alfredian circle" only one is known by name, Bishop Wærferth, translator of the *Dialogues*. No authors have been suggested for the other texts that we now know were not written by Alfred. Unable to name others in this circle, much less link specific translations to them, we should avoid the term "Alfredian circle," and others that are its companions (such as "Alfredian translation"). Even the term "Alfredian" is unsatisfactory. It may describe a work that Alfred himself is thought to have written; or it may indicate a text that is generally datable to the ninth century and is possibly—but not conclusively—linked to his court. Given this vagueness, "Alfredian" and related terms will be avoided in this work.

Second, to understand Alfred's contribution to his translations, what we might call his "originality," we should know precisely with which Latin texts he worked. The *Consolation of Philosophy* and the *Pastoral Care* were very popular works in the early Middle Ages and were often transmitted in corrupt or otherwise faulty copies. In most cases, we have only a vague idea of the quality of Alfred's Latin sources; he may have known the works of Gregory and Augustine in good or only in incomplete, error-filled versions. We may never succeed in comparing Alfred's translations to their Latin sources so that we can note his additions and deletions. Although we might want to agree with Kirby that we discern "the personality of the king" through his additions and insertions into texts,[46] our scanty knowledge of Alfred's sources prohibits sweeping claims about the changes he may have made or the personality they may reveal.

Third, we must exercise caution in setting the chronology of Alfred's works. Neither Asser nor Alfred indicated the order in which the works were produced, and the sequence has yet to be established with precision. Manuscripts of some of Alfred's translations are dated significantly later than the period in which Alfred himself worked, so we must allow considerable time for corruption and interpolation in the years between the text's composition and the dates from which the manuscripts survive. However, the *Pastoral Care* is known to have been the first of the translations; it was perhaps preceded by compilation of the law code, which did not depend exclusively on Latin sources. The translations of works by Boethius and Augustine appear, for many reasons, to have been undertaken at nearly the same time; the relationship of the translation of the psalms to the other texts is uncertain. Without asserting a fixed chronology, the following chapters will first discuss Alfred's law code and then the *Pastoral Care*, the *Consolation of Philosophy*, the *Soliloquies*, and finally the *Paris Psalter*.

Chapter Two

King Alfred's Law Code

Alfred's law code was probably issued early in his administration, in the late 880s or early in the 890s, and so represents one of his earliest literary endeavors, perhaps his first.[1] To consider the laws from a literary point of view may at first seem strange or inappropriate, for they are not what we consider literary prose; rather than a discussion of ideas, they resemble a catalogue or a list. However, Alfred introduced the law code with an extensive prologue setting forth his concepts of law and lawgiving. This introduction includes translations of scriptural passages, chiefly from the Book of Exodus, and is extremely important both for the history of English law and for the study of Alfred's use of literature.

Following this introduction is a collection of statutes issued by earlier kings and those promulgated by Alfred himself.[2] Alone among his writings, therefore, the law code is not a reworking of classical or patristic sources.[3] It is instead a theoretical and practical recasting of the Anglo-Saxon legal tradition. By publishing a set of laws, the first issued in England in a century, Alfred renewed a tradition that had lapsed in the legal, political, and social chaos that followed the Viking invasions. His code has been called "a public display of a king's royal power" which "provided an opportunity for him to express his political and ideological aspirations in legal form."[4]

But the political and legal importance of the code does not overshadow its literary significance. Alfred did more than merely gather earlier codes and, with the advice of his counselors, adapt them to his own needs. He also interpreted the laws as part of a tradition of government in which the king's role assumed new importance. His code reveals his grasp of the power of lawgiving and of preserving law in writing. It manifests a vision of kingship and authority later elaborated in Alfred's translations of theological and philosophical texts.

The Manuscript Tradition

The authenticity of Alfred's laws, at least as a collection sponsored if not actually written by the king, seems never to have been seriously questioned.[5] The introduction claims that Alfred issued the code, and although other contemporary sources—such as Asser's *Life*—do not mention his laws, no one has doubted that they originated with Alfred. Two complete manuscripts and four fragments survive. The law text in the earliest manuscript (Cambridge, Corpus Christi College 173), was written in the mid-tenth century;[6] the other complete copy, included in the *Textus Roffensis*, was written at Rochester in the first quarter of the twelfth century.[7] Together with the fragments, the complete manuscripts suggest that the law code circulated widely.[8] In the twelfth century Alfred's code was translated from Old English into Latin and was included in the compilation known as the *Quadripartitus*.[9]

Because Alfred based his collection on earlier laws, the study of his code brings us into contact with almost all the surviving Anglo-Saxon law collections.[10] Those that predate Alfred's laws are the laws of Ine (688–694) and the laws of early Kentish kings, Ethelberht (602–3?), Hlothhere and Eadric (673–685?), and Wihtred (695).[11] The manuscript traditions of these codes, Alfred's laws, and later Anglo-Saxon compilations have recently been thoroughly reexamined.[12]

Alfred's debt to these earlier collections remains unclear.[13] Some of the collections which predate Alfred's code, and which he drew on, are preserved independently of his code. Because the laws of Kentish kings, including Ethelberht, are preserved in the *Textus Roffensis*, we can compare Alfred's revision of Ethelberht's laws to the version of that code in the *Textus Roffensis* and determine the extent to which Alfred reshaped his source.[14] The laws of Offa and Ine, however, do not exist in separate manuscripts, and are known to us only because Alfred incorporated them into his code. Ine's laws seem to be an appendix to Alfred's collection and are usually edited separately. This is an unfortunate practice, for it implies that Ine's laws, as Alfred received them, constitute the code as Ine himself issued it some two hundred years before Alfred ruled. Historians may reasonably suppose that during those two centuries Ine's laws absorbed interpolations and additions, so that the version known to Alfred must have been considerably altered from the laws as Ine promulgated them. As Milton Haight Turk pointed out, all manuscripts show that Ine's laws form "an intrinsic, inseparable part of [Alfred's] own code."[15] Without independent evidence of Ine's code, we cannot determine the form in which Alfred first received it.

Alfred's Laws and the Anglo-Saxon Legal Tradition

Alfred's laws synthesize many traditions, including the Mosaic law of Scripture, the synodical records of the early church, and, most important, the written law of his own nation. Anglo-Saxon law was mainly customary and unwritten, a kind of law very different from the written code that is the common form of law today.[16] Penalties or punishments for violations which occurred frequently were known to a group of counselors whose duty it was to preserve in memory the tradition of legal practice. In Alfred's day laws were written only on those infrequent occasions "when a custom had to be altered, or clarified, or emphasized." Early English lawbooks, therefore, were "at once very particular and precise and very fragmentary": they concerned themselves with those cases that required special consideration, or that raised issues that were not treated by the orally preserved customary law.[17]

Adding to the complexity of Anglo-Saxon law was its regional character. The law was not only "for the most part unwritten," but also "varied from district to district."[18] We know that Alfred gathered Mercian and Kentish as well as West Saxon codes, "the most just laws that he could find."[19] Thus he created a new concept of "English" law. Although the laws refer to Alfred as "King of the West Saxons"—a title appropriate to an early stage of his reign—the code was intended to apply to a whole nation and attests to "the new political unity forced upon the various English people by the struggle against the Danes."[20] By publishing a "national" code, Alfred attempted to unify written law, bring older practices into conformity with the customs of his own time, and simultaneously place that law in the broader context of all law, divine as well as human.

The Structure of Alfred's Law Code

Mindful of the impact his laws would have, Alfred skillfully manipulated tradition while compiling them. The complex structure of his code reflects its synthetic purposes. In the oldest manuscript (Cambridge, Corpus Christi College 173) the collection is divided into 120 books, an organizational design which reflects a literary tradition rather than a logical necessity. The division into 120 chapters has been seen as a commemoration of the age of Moses, the archetypal lawgiver, said to have died at age 120.[21] Some such symbolic significance does seem to have motivated the chapter divisions, for they do not correspond to logical divisions of the subject matter. The headings of some chapters concern two or even three different provisions. According to Turk, no precedent exists for the use of chapter headings in earlier collections.[22] Alfred was likely to have used them to give his laws a superstructure, a comprehensive design and coherence.

The lengthy introduction that precedes the statutes themselves discusses Alfred's theory of law, the precedents for his code, and his purpose in compiling laws for his people.[23] The sections of the introduction have been numbered by modern editors from 1 through 49, a numerical system not found in any manuscript but useful in distinguishing the four parts of the introduction. Paragraphs 1–48, without division, form the so-called "historical introduction" and contain translations of the Mosaic law; paragraphs 49 to 49.5 are again scriptural; paragraphs 49.6–8, numbered 1 (the first of the 120 chapters in the manuscript), concern the dissemination of law throughout all lands of the early Church; paragraphs 49.9–10, unnumbered and known as the "introduction proper," concern law in Alfred's own age. These sections form a coherent, closely argued preface to Alfred's law code. Following the fourth part of the introduction are the laws themselves, divided into three collections: 2–39, miscellaneous laws; 40–43, laws concerning bodily injuries; and 44–120, the laws of Ine.[24]

The introduction to Alfred's Code.   Alfred's introduction is one of his most important and interesting prefaces, but it has gone untranslated in the standard reference works. Attenborough omitted most of the introduction in his translation because he saw it "as having no bearing on Anglo-Saxon law," a dismaying judgment and a gross underestimation of the text.[25] Small sections of the introduction are translated by Whitelock and by Keynes and Lapidge, but it is incomprehensible that this extremely important and interesting material is otherwise not available to a general reading audience.[26]

Paragraphs 1–49.5.   Alfred's code begins with laws from ecclesiastical sources—the Decalogue, or Ten Commandments, and Hebrew law as handed down in the Book of Exodus—and then explains the process by which Old Testament law was modified for Christian times and established as law for all Christians by early church councils. These paragraphs are the only portion of Alfred's code translated from a Latin source. Although we cannot be certain which form of the Bible Alfred knew, his extracts from Exodus closely resemble those found in an Irish canonical collection known as the *Liber ex Lege Moysi*.[27] He includes a portion of the Ten Commandments, omitting the second and parts of the fourth and the tenth, and then quotes extensive statutes from the Book of Exodus that support the Decalogue.[28]

Most of the provisions reflect Old Testament teaching, but in paragraph 49 Alfred effects a transition from the Old Law to the New, which he presents as the law of God Himself. He points out the lack of conflict between the Mosaic laws and the New Dispensation, the law of Christ, which Christ taught with "mercy and humility." Alfred then translates what is known as the "Apostolic letter" (Acts 15:23–29). This letter, which promulgated the Mosaic law, was sent by the Apostles in Jerusalem to the Gentiles of Antioch, Syria, and Cilicia, urging them to abstain from the worship of idols, from eating unclean foods, and from unchastity. The introduction balances the justice and severity of the Old Law with the love and mercy of Christ as exemplified in the New Law. The letter concludes with a version of the "Greatest Commandment" or "Golden Rule": "What you wish that other men may not do to you, do not to other men."[29]

Paragraphs 49.6–8. Having translated and paraphrased Mosaic law, Alfred bridges the Old and New Testament theories of law with further discussion of the "Golden Rule":

A man can think on this one sentence alone, that he judges each one rightly; he has need of no other law-books. Let him bethink him that he judge to no man what he would not that he judged to him, if he were giving the judgment on him.[30]

As Turk comments, this precept touches on "the spirit of all law and justice, the underlying principle of all lawgiving."[31] Alfred then joins his survey of scriptural legal precedent to his own time, beginning with the early Christian period, when "many peoples had received the faith of Christ" and "many synods were assembled throughout all the earth, and likewise throughout the English people." Early Christian synods serve as a model for the synods that established customary law in England: the people agreed "that secular lords might with their permission receive without sin compensation in money for almost every misdeed at the first offense, which compensation they then fixed." Thus Alfred invokes ancient origins for the legal system of his time, when compensation for all crimes but one took the form of fines. The sole exception was treachery to one's lord. For that crime the people "dared not declare any mercy, because Almighty God adjudged none for those who scorned him, nor did Christ" (49.7). The laws, once approved by the English synods, were preserved in "synod books" which recorded "the compensations for many human misdeeds" for all posterity (49.8); from such books Alfred drew his own code.[32]

Paragraphs 49.9–10. The series of his own laws now begins:

Now I, King Alfred, have collected these laws, and have given orders for copies to be made of many of those which our predecessors observed and which I myself approved of. But many of those I did not approve of I have rejected, with the advice of my councillors, and I have ordered changes to be introduced into others.[33]

Alfred's debt to tradition was selective; he was not only a lawgiver but a power who determined, in consultation with others, which laws of earlier generations would be preserved. The introduction to his code concludes by listing the sources of the laws which follow: those from the "time of my kinsmen" (meaning Alfred's own immediate predecessors); the laws of Ine; the laws of Offa; and the laws of Ethelberht.

Alfred's, Ethelberht's, and Ine's laws. Numbered 2–39 in the manuscript (actually comprising 43 separate provisions),[34] the first group of laws is a miscellaneous collection. Presumably Offa's laws form part of this section, since Alfred names him as one of his sources (Introduction 49.9, 63), but Offa's laws do not survive in a separate collection and are not set apart in Alfred's code. The range of crimes covered here is extensive, but the primary concerns are personal injury and property. The most important offense is breaking one's promise or oath; anyone who did not keep his oath and pledge was required to give up his arms, go into the king's prison for forty days, and perform ecclesiastical penance as prescribed by the bishop (1.1–8, 63–65).

This reference to a bishop's role in the penalty assessed by secular authority calls our attention to the cooperation of church and state prescribed by Alfred's laws. One of his code's chief characteristics is the extent to which the church was placed under the secular government's protection, receiving secular assistance in the enforcement of ecclesiastical law. The protection of the church by the secular authority is stronger in this section of Alfred's code—the section that he shaped the most, and the section that reflects practices of his own time—than it is in the earlier collections. The cooperation between church and state became even more evident in the later Anglo-Saxon period, when Wulfstan, Bishop of London and Archbishop of York (d. 1023), framed legislation for King Ethelred and King Cnut.[35]

Examples of this cooperation are numerous. One guilty of breaking an oath who escaped from prison and was not apprehended was to be "excommunicated from all the churches of Christ" (1.7, 65). The right of the church to give sanctuary to the accused was carefully defined and regulated; if the community should need the church while a fugitive was sequestered there, he was to be moved to another building which, for the fugitive's protection, was to have no more doors than the church (5–5.1, 67). Theft during Lent, or on Christmas, Easter, Rogation Days, or Sunday, required double compensation (5.5, 67). The rules for fasting during Lent were protected; violating them required 120 shillings compensation (40.2, 83). Theft from churches was severely punished: not only was compensation required, but the thief was also to lose the hand with which the act was committed (6, 67–69).

Alfred's code reflects the "very particular and precise" nature of the written laws and penalties for unusual offenses. For example, if a man cut wood on land belonging to another, he was to pay a set price for each tree. If a man accidentally killed another by letting a tree fall on him, the tree was to be given to the dead man's kin (12, 13; 71). Another peculiar provision, dealt with at some length, specifies penalties for the man who injures another in the way he carries his spear over his shoulder. If a spear carrier should accidentally transfix another on his spear, the offender was to pay the *wergeld*, the value of the life of the injured, but was not to be fined. However, if the offender acted knowingly, he was to pay *wergeld* as well as a fine, provided that the spear was "higher than the butt end of the shaft." If the spear were level, "the man with the spear [was not to be] regarded as responsible for causing danger," presumably because he was carrying his weapon correctly (36.1–2; 79–81). Such a provision is so specific that it must have been written to deal with a specific incident;

the matter would not have arisen often and would not have been customarily in dispute; hence it was preserved in writing for future reference.

The second part of the laws, chapters 40–43, is a revision of Ethelberht's code concerning personal injuries; it comprises 34 sections in Attenborough's edition.[36] Alfred's version of these laws, compared to the version preserved in the *Textus Roffensis*, shows that he attempted to revise the older code. The laws concerning personal injuries incorporate a traditional medieval catalogue of the parts of the body, assigning fines according to the bodily member injured. The order of fines is not perfectly systematic in the source, Ethelberht's code; and even in Alfred's revision, portions of the code depart from the head-to-toe regularity usually followed in such catalogues.[37] Nevertheless, Alfred's version is more systematic than the material from which he worked. Turk claims that Alfred revised a somewhat disorganized and random text to conform to "his sense of order and to his views of literary propriety."[38] This point is worth stressing, for it suggests that Alfred was concerned about form and organization not only because they could facilitate administration, but also because they were logical and right for literature.

The code first lists injuries to the head—gashes to the skull, and loss of eyes, ears, nose, and teeth. Compensation for striking off a nose (60 shillings) was twice that for striking off an ear, unless in the latter case the hearing was stopped. The compensation for each finger differed, and likewise for each toe. The code is not perfectly consistent—eye injuries are included in two places—but Alfred's revision brings greater harmony and plan to the collection than it had in its earlier form.[39] Alfred almost always altered the penalty assigned each offense, usually by increasing the compensatory fine. For example, Ethelberht's code demanded 12 shillings compensation if an ear was struck off, Alfred's, 30; and for loss of hearing, Ethelberht demanded 25 shillings, Alfred 60.[40]

The final section of the laws of Alfred, chapters 44–120, consists of Ine's laws, an extensive collection of 76 separate provisions which include a large range of offenses against persons and property.[41] The laws of Ine are not merely a "supplement" or appendix to Alfred's collection, or an "aid" to it.[42] The integral relationship of the two codes was first noticed by Turk, who pointed out that although earlier sections of Alfred's laws are extremely detailed, they scarcely mention certain important offenses, in particular those concerning theft and stolen goods. Alfred omitted these crimes from the earlier chapters, according to Turk, because they were discussed in detail in Ine's code, which regards thievery "from every imaginable point of view." On the other hand, Ine's laws say relatively little about homicide, which the earlier chapters, especially the miscellaneous laws, discuss in detail.[43]

Alfred's own revisions of Ine's code may not have been extensive. The introduction to the code was retained as the forty-fourth of the 120 chapters of Alfred's collection. It begins:

I, Ine, by the grace of God king of Wessex, with the advice and instruction of my father Cenred, and my bishop Hædde, and my bishop Eorcenwold, and with all my ealdormen and the chief councillors of my people, and with a great assembly of the servants of God, have been taking counsel for the salvation of our souls and for the security of our realm, in order that just law and just decrees may be established and ensured throughout our nation, so that no ealdormen nor subjects of ours may henceforth pervert these our decrees.[44]

Had he undertaken a thorough revision of Ine's code, Alfred would no doubt have omitted or altered the reference in the introduction to the adoption of the "just law and just decrees" by a "great assembly." Alfred's own prologue already made reference to such assemblies and the "synod books" which recorded their views. Further evidence that Alfred did not greatly revise the laws of Ine as they descended to him is seen in those provisions found earlier in Alfred's laws that contradict the laws found in the present section. For example, Ine set a fine of 120 shillings for breaking into the king's premises or those of a bishop; Alfred also set a fine of 120 shillings for breaking into the king's premises, but 90 shillings for violating an archbishop's quarters, and only 60 for transgressing those of a bishop.[45] Had Alfred revised Ine's code, such duplication and contradiction would presumably have been eliminated. However, lacking independent manuscript evidence of Ine's laws, we cannot determine the extent of Alfred's revision of them.

Relation of Alfred's Law Code to Other Texts

Given their nature and purpose, Alfred's laws cannot be said to represent his literary skills or ambitions extensively. The laws may

have been Alfred's first literary act, undertaken before he conceived of
the program of translations for which he is famous. Yet we must see
that there is a harmony between the publication of his laws, with its
elaborate and distinctly literary form, and his translations. In the
laws, as in the other texts, Alfred consciously reshaped tradition as he
became part of it. With the laws of English kings, just as with the
texts of Boethius, Augustine, and Gregory the Great, and with the
Book of Psalms, Alfred set himself a task that entailed translation,
reconstruction, and the application of a transforming intelligence.

The commentary and observations that Alfred incorporated into his
laws show his sensitivity to tradition and his grasp of his own duties,
and are the strongest signs of the king's interest in using literature
and writing to create and preserve social order and harmony. His
translations discuss the theory of government in greater detail, but
none presents an overview of the tradition of authority comparable to
that in the introduction to the laws. One theme that runs through all
Alfred's translations, and that is discussed nowhere more forcefully
and clearly than in the laws, is kingship. Although Alfred's idea of
the king and the king's power reflects the influence of Carolingian and
Frankish models, he surpassed all but a few of his predecessors in using law and learning to define and exalt his office. All his translations
express the view that the king was the center of authority and was
also expected to be the source of wisdom.

In the introduction to his laws Alfred's concern with authority
manifests itself in statements about the obedience and loyalty due
one's lord. He claims that all Christian people, including of course
the English, declared that only one crime could not be compensated,
and that was treachery to a lord. The traitor deserved only death;
Christ himself refused him mercy, and, Alfred adds, "charged everyone to love his lord as himself." This charge is a curious recasting of
the "Great Commandment," Christ's words in the Gospel of Matthew
(Matthew 22): "You shall love the Lord your God with all your heart,
and with all your soul, and with all your mind" (v. 37), and "You
shall love your neighbor as yourself" (v. 39).[46] Alfred transforms the
command to love the "Lord your God" with sincerity into a demand
for unquestioning obedience to authority. Such obedience, demanded
by the king's supreme power and expressed by unswerving loyalty to
one's lord, is asserted not only in the prologue to his laws but also in
the *Pastoral Care* and the *Consolation of Philosophy*. As Loyn states, "the
ideas of Christian lordship that one finds . . . so strongly expressed"

in this prologue reflect Alfred's belief that the king was "expected to rule, and also to define law."[47]

We must also situate Alfred's laws in the context of other kinds of historical writing, in particular the *Anglo-Saxon Chronicle*, a work which is bound in the same manuscript as the oldest copy of Alfred's laws (Cambridge, Corpus Christi College 173). Like the laws, the *Chronicle* prefaces Alfred's reign with a synthetic view of history. Just as the introduction to Alfred's code traces his own laws and lawgiving authority to Moses, the *Chronicle* begins by tracing the royal genealogy to the early Christian and Roman worlds, "In the year when 494 years had passed from Christ's birth."[48] In reaching to the distant past in this way, both texts seek to augment the king's power and prestige by asserting precedents for his authority. The *Chronicle* was, scholars believe, compiled under the force of Frankish example; Alfred's laws may also reflect continental influence.[49]

The concept of kingship that Alfred acquired from his reading informs his writing to a remarkable extent. Literature was not the source of his royal power, but he made it an important reinforcement for the ideals of kingship and loyalty that held his England together. The law code is our first sign of his faith in the power of literature— in written documents—to propagate values and to forge a unified consciousness among his people.

Chapter Three

The *Pastoral Care*: Translation of Gregory the Great

King Alfred's translation of Pope Gregory the Great's *Liber Regulae Pastoralis* takes its customary modern English title from the opening words of the Latin text, "Pastoralis curae me pondera."[1] It is usually known as the *Pastoral Care*, but the literal translation, The Book of Pastoral Rule, more accurately suggests the purpose of Gregory's book, which was to serve as a guide for pastors, a guide modeled on rules for the religious life of monastics and for the secular clergy.[2] Alfred's Anglo-Saxon title was *Hirdeboc*, the Shepherd's Book, and he intended it not only as a handbook or guidebook, but also as a vehicle for launching a program of educational renewal without precedent in English history.[3] In this discussion we will use the standard modern title, *Pastoral Care*, when referring to the translation, and *Regula Pastoralis* when referring to Gregory's original.

The first of Alfred's translations, the *Pastoral Care* is also both an exercise in practical instruction and a scrupulous examination of human behavior. Although it is not an inquiry into abstractions comparable to Boethius's *Consolation of Philosophy* or Augustine's *Soliloquies*, the *Pastoral Care* is more richly theoretical than most of its readers have realized. Alfred's other translations better illuminate the role of wisdom in society and the need for leaders to be learned, but none illustrates the aims of his educational program and his methods of achieving them better than the *Pastoral Care*.[4]

The Manuscript Tradition

Few have seriously questioned that Alfred himself translated the *Pastoral Care*, although the role of his helpers in producing the text was evidently large. Alfred could have had little scholarly experience in the early 890s, when the translation was undertaken, and scarcely could have managed this massive project—the longest of all his translations—alone.[5] His *Pastoral Care* was more faithful to its original than his other translations were to be, and accordingly was less a vehicle for his own thoughts than they were. Alfred seems to have wished to adhere closely to Gregory's original and to impart its meaning as directly as possible. We can understand why Alfred did not alter the *Pastoral Care* substantially when we consider the extreme good sense and the practicality of the text's advice for spiritual leaders; its extraordinary dependence on Scripture—which it quotes some 485 times—must also have commanded the king's respect.[6] The *Pastoral Care* stood less in need of revision, simplification, or clarification for Alfred's audience than did the elaborate theoretical treatises of Boethius and Augustine.[7]

Alfred attached two prefaces to the text. The longer, well-known prose preface describes Alfred's wishes for the publication of the text and declares his intent to send a copy "to every bishopric in my kingdom."[8] We should not underestimate the technical difficulties created by Alfred's plans to distribute the work. Kenneth Sisam calculates that at least ten copies were required, a tall order for even a large scriptorium (copying center), much less a scribal center in England in Alfred's time.[9] Thus the *Pastoral Care*, recopied many times, acquired an extensive manuscript tradition; it survives, in whole or in part, in six manuscripts, more than any of his other works. One complete manuscript, and a fragment of another, date from 890–897, and are the earliest copies of any of Alfred's translations.[10]

The prose preface resembles a form letter: in one manuscript a blank was left for the name of the bishop to whom the copy was to be sent; another names Bishop Wærferth of Worcester, directing the text to that destination.[11] The manuscripts show that the publication of the text was not accomplished in a single scriptorium. The preface in the oldest manuscript was written in one scriptorium and then joined with the text, which had been written in another, before the book was sent to the intended bishop.[12] Alfred attached immense importance to this undertaking, including with each copy an "æstal" (probably a bookmark) worth the considerable sum of fifty mancuses and directing that the book was never to leave the bishop's church unless he wished to have it copied. Alfred had reason to issue such a caution, for the libraries in his day were not usually stationary collections; volumes apparently were lent to other libraries with some regularity and were not always returned.[13]

The manuscript evidence attests to the popularity of the *Pastoral*

Care in another way. Surviving manuscripts are distributed over nearly two centuries; they show that the language was adapted or modernized as the text circulated.[14] Forms in two eleventh-century manuscripts have been altered and the spellings of Alfred's day replaced with later forms.[15] In the early eleventh century the preface was revised and the changes were entered in the oldest manuscript, that which was contemporary with Alfred, by Archbishop Wulfstan, the leading figure of the late Anglo-Saxon church.[16]

The Source: Gregory's *Liber Regulae Pastoralis*

Gregory the Great's *Liber Regulae Pastoralis* survives in some five hundred Latin manuscripts, eleven of Anglo-Saxon provenance.[17] The oldest of the Latin manuscripts, now in Troyes, contains two nearly contemporary versions of the text, one believed to be Gregory's original version, written in Rome about 590, and another adding corrections to that text, probably under the Pope's supervision before his death in 604.[18] Significant differences are found in the Latin editions, as we would expect in a text revised by its author and so frequently recopied. The variants make it possible to classify the Latin versions into families and by this method to determine the form of the text known to Alfred.

Recent research shows that Alfred is likely to have known a corrected rather than an uncorrected version of the text. The version printed in the *Patrologia Latina*, relied on by many scholars who study Alfred's text, is actually Gregory's corrected version; the edition by Westhoff, also cited in important studies of Alfred's translation, likewise represents only a small part of the manuscript evidence.[19] If we would know with any certainty how Alfred's translation compares with the Latin original, we must know more about the Latin text itself; we cannot justly estimate Alfred's skill and success in translating the text until we know the text he translated and the textual tradition within which he worked.[20]

The importance of Gregory's *Liber Regulae Pastoralis* in the Middle Ages can scarcely be exaggerated. Its popularity derives both from its immediate application—its concern with the qualities of the good pastor—and the obvious relevance of Gregory's comments about the pastoral office to the office of kingship. The first of these concerns was primary for Gregory, who completed the text (begun in Constantinople) when he was considering a call to the papacy in 590. A former abbot of St. Andrew's monastery in Rome (one of seven which he founded), Gregory was made a high-ranking administrator of the Roman Church. He left the monastic life with deep regret to assume these public responsibilities and later the papacy.[21] The tension between the life of contemplative retirement and the life of an active church leader—the *vita contemplativa* and the *vita activa*—dominated much of his writing, including the *Regula Pastoralis*, which, according to Jeffrey Richards, was "in large part devoted to describing how to reconcile the two types of life" and to creating "a pastoral episcopate, trained in preaching and teaching."[22] Gregory circulated the work among his bishops, much as Alfred did later. The work was translated into Greek in Gregory's own lifetime but was not translated into another vernacular until Alfred undertook his project.[23]

Unlike the other texts that Alfred translated, the *Regula Pastoralis* had a long history in England. The English church had a special affinity for Gregory, who commissioned Augustine, prior of St. Andrews, and later at Canterbury, to go to England and, tradition has it, to take the *Regula Pastoralis* with him. Gregory was revered as the pope who sought to save English Christianity; his biography, the first life of the saint, was written in Whitby, in northern England.[24] The *Regula Pastoralis* was known to Bede and recommended by him, and was quoted in his *Ecclesiastical History*.[25] Alcuin, writing to an archbishop in 796, urged that it be reread often; since the *Regula Pastoralis* outlined different classes of the faithful and advised the pastor how to counsel each, it was, Alcuin claimed, an invaluable reference for preachers.[26]

Equally significant for King Alfred was the popularity of the text in the Carolingian church. Reform councils called by Charlemagne in 813 made study of the text obligatory for all bishops, and subsequent decrees incorporated whole sections of the text.[27] Later, under Archbishop Hincmar of Reims (d. 882), it became traditional for bishops to hold copies of the text at their consecration.[28]

Carolingian bishops as well as Alfred and his bishops shared the need for pastoral instruction of preachers and teachers. They also urgently needed leaders among the people to help achieve unity, social harmony, and peace. In applying the text to questions of secular office, the Carolingians and Alfred mirrored Gregory's interest in kingship and his awareness of the common ground shared by kings and bishops.[29] The *Pastoral Care* supported one of the most important medieval attitudes toward secular authority, namely that it could not be separated from the divine; to disobey one's lord was to sin against God.

Kingship is linked to God throughout Alfred's text, wherein one word, *dryhten*, designates both Christ and the secular lord.[30] For this reason the *Pastoral Care* may be called a treatise about power. Analyzing from many perspectives the relations of ruler to the ruled, it reminds the ruler that he must constantly examine his worthiness to exercise authority and must exercise power not for himself but for the benefit of others. Two lessons are said to emerge on "every page" of the *Regula Pastoralis*: first, that the ruler's morality is the basis of his authority; second, that ruling is a "professional occupation" requiring training and constant self-examination.[31] The text describes Gregory's image of the ideal bishop,[32] but its theme, larger than the bishop's education, is the challenge to righteous action posed by the temptations of power.

Alfred's Preface to the *Pastoral Care*

Alfred retained Gregory's preface to the *Regula Pastoralis* but preceded it with two new prefaces of his own, one in verse and one in prose. The brief verse preface merely identifies Alfred as the author and asserts that Augustine brought the book with him from Rome at Gregory's command. It does not refer to Alfred's educational program, except to say that he commanded his scribes "to produce more such copies from the exemplar, so that he could send them to his bishops," some of whom knew no Latin and so needed texts in their own language.[33]

The prose preface is without question the most discussed of Alfred's writings. Frequently reprinted in anthologies introducing students to Old English, it remains our richest source of information about Alfred's concept of learning, the purposes behind his program of translation, and his methods for disseminating translated works throughout his kingdom. Unlike virtually everything else Alfred wrote, the prose preface has no counterpart in Latin. Therefore, it has special interest as a specimen of original English composition. Its complex manuscript tradition supports the claims made in both prefaces about Alfred's plans to circulate the work.[34]

Interpretations of the preface are many; studies of Alfred's *Pastoral Care* itself are few. Indeed, scholars have been content to analyze the plans for educational renewal outlined in the preface without considering the manner in which the *Pastoral Care* exemplifies them. And too few readers of the preface link it to the work that follows or explore the connection between Gregory's purpose and Alfred's execution of it.

Of the many detailed analyses of the preface available, the most illuminating is T.A. Shippey's discussion of "wealth and wisdom" in the text.[35] Shippey divides the preface into five sections, each concerned with a specific period of English history. In the first, Alfred looks back from the impoverished conditions of his own age to the glories of the late seventh century, traditionally regarded as the zenith of learning in early England, a period of wealth and wisdom. Alfred then evokes the days of his boyhood, the second period, with images of churches once rich in treasures and books, and later ransacked by the invaders. Owing to a lack of English translations, the books could not be understood; hence this period was a time of wealth without wisdom.

In the third period—when Alfred came to the throne in 871—neither wealth nor wisdom was to be found. In the fourth, the time of the writing of the preface, Alfred sees at least some learning, some indication of wisdom; he himself demonstrates wisdom in his plan to "turn into the language that we can all understand certain books which are the most necessary for all men to know," so that all "freeborn" young men will be able to read English, and those who advance to orders will read Latin as well. In Alfred's own time, as Shippey tells us, at least some wisdom flourishes—wisdom enough to know what will be necessary to recapture the wisdom of the past. Finally, Alfred completes the historical scheme by looking ahead to a time when both wisdom and wealth will be restored to his kingdom.[36]

As an alternative to Shippey's historical analysis, Paul E. Szarmach stresses the theme of wisdom in the text and the influence of Church fathers, Augustine in particular, on Alfred's thought. Szarmach argues that the preface is about wisdom as *sapientia*, and that Alfred's "major theme is the pursuit of wisdom and his minor theme the decay of Latinity."[37] This analysis directs our attention away from the preface as a historical record to its use of traditional Christian literary themes, in this case the "divergence between the appearance of belief and the reality of behavior." Another as yet inadequately explored approach to the riches of the preface is an analysis of the literary traditions from which it borrows.[38] Jennifer Morrish's analysis has recently demonstrated the deeply conventional nature of much of Alfred's rhetoric, which has impressed so many scholars as revolutionary.[39]

The preface is skillfully, even masterfully composed. The periodic sweep of its first sentence reveals the carefully arranged subdivisions of Alfred's society and the role assigned to learning in each. The role of the king in revitalizing the decayed tradition is especially well developed:

And I would have it known that very often it has come to my mind what men of learning formerly existed throughout England, both in religious and secular orders; and how there were happy times then throughout England; and how the kings who had authority over this people obeyed God and his representatives; and how they both maintained their peace, morality, and power at home and at the same time increased their territory abroad; and how they prospered both in warfare and in wisdom; and how zealous the sacred orders were both in teaching and in learning and in all the services they rendered to God; and how those from abroad sought wisdom and learning in this country; and how these days we would have to seek such things from outside, if we wished to acquire them. (3)

The design of this sentence is worth close attention. Remembering the achievements of a bygone era, Alfred recalls the presence of learned men "throughout England" and equates that abundance with "happy times." In particular, he recalls that the kings, obedient to God and His messengers, not only maintained peace at home but extended their realms, and thus were successful "both in warfare and wisdom"—a more potent and telling combination, perhaps, than the "wealth and wisdom" Shippey analyzes. The harmony between church and state, the balance achieved by earlier rulers between military and moral excellence, and their success in promoting both domestic tranquillity and conquest, constituted an ideal to which Alfred aspired. He notes that simultaneously the religious orders were eager to teach and to learn, and to perform holy services as well. So excellent was this civilization that it was a model to foreign scholars who arrived in England to study.

Having described this golden age, Alfred turns with devastating effect to the weaknesses of his own period. He observes ruefully that those who wished to acquire wisdom, learning, and instruction were forced to seek them outside the country. Surely this was the gravest loss of all: once a beacon to other nations, England now had to seek their guidance for leadership in learning. Alfred excuses the learned men of earlier times who left books in Latin because they did not expect "that men would ever become so careless and that learning would decay like this."

Recalling how God's law was translated first into Hebrew, then Greek, and then Latin, he concludes that "it seems better to me—if it seems so to you—that we too should turn into the language that we can all understand certain books most necessary for all men to know" (7). The invocation of the sacred languages recalls the introduction Alfred wrote for his law code; here, too, he seeks a precedent in Scripture for his program of translation. Latin should be taught in the kingdom to those who wish to take holy orders, he notes, and "all the free-born young men now in England who have the means to apply themselves to it" should be set to learning how to read English. Despite the good sense of Alfred's preface, we should hesitate to believe that he expected schoolboys to read the *Pastoral Care* or that he had "all men" in mind when he decided to translate Gregory's book. Rather, Alfred began his educational program where necessary, at the beginning, first commanding that his bishops read the text and apply its wisdom in their dealings. From them Gregory's wisdom would flow to other pastors, and from them to their charges.

In reading the *Pastoral Care* itself, we may put the injunctions of Alfred's preface in the context of Gregory's own concerns; however, we cannot assume that the two authors addressed similar audiences, even though both audiences were primarily episcopal. Gregory sought to balance the active and contemplative lives, and to harmonize the wisdom gained in prayer and contemplation with acts of Christian leadership. For Alfred the problem was somewhat different. His pairing of "warfare and wisdom" reflects his own concern with harmonizing life and learning. Both in the preface and in the *Pastoral Care* he sought to introduce the knowledge gained in contemplation into a world of strife and struggle, where learning and the desire for wisdom had scarcely room to survive.

Alfred's Translation

Until we identify the edition of Gregory's text known to Alfred, generalizing about his adaptation of his source is dangerous. Yet scholars unanimously agree that Alfred's translation is conservative, following Gregory's original so closely that the differences between

them—especially when compared to Alfred's apparent divergence
from other Latin texts he translated—are relatively minor. In his preface Alfred states that he sometimes translated his material "word for
word, sometimes sense for sense" (7). This distinction in approaches
to translation—which we might identify as close translation versus
paraphrase—appears in Gregory's writings as well as in Asser's *Life* of
Alfred.[40] Alfred usually translates "sense for sense" rather than literally, a result that strikes many as unsatisfactory and unadventurous.[41]

We do well to remember that the *Regula Pastoralis* is not an open-
ended text, but rather one bound by a specific structure and careful
subdivision and taxonomy, very different in this regard from the texts
of Augustine and Boethius which Alfred translated. One might assume that Alfred hesitated to alter the text out of reverence to Gregory's authority and importance, but in his translation of the *Soliloquies*
Alfred evidently felt very free to transform extensively the text of Augustine, no less an authority than Gregory.[42] He had opportunity to
digress on matters of special interest to himself in Gregory's text, had
he so desired. Perhaps Alfred's reasons for not expanding on the text
had nothing to do with its elaborate structure. In the early phases of
his program of translation he may have worked conservatively; but his
fidelity to Gregory's original may mean only that Alfred was preoccupied and had little chance to reflect on this document and enlarge on
its ideas.

Alfred did introduce some changes to the text. He added incidental
information and explication, as he did in other translations, as background for his readers. Hence, he indicates a name of a book of the
Bible where Gregory did not (275); he specifies that Gregory's "Veri-
tas" or Truth is Christ, and that the 'holy Church" is the "assembly
of Christ's people" (43). Generally more specific in his references to
Scripture than his source was, Alfred notes books of the Bible with
special frequency after chapter 36, and after chapter 53 begins including the numbers of the psalms he quotes. Alfred himself probably did
not know Scripture well enough to supply these references unaided
(although he did translate the first fifty psalms). These additions
would seem to be the work of his helpers. Perhaps because different
scholars worked on different parts of the translation, applying different methods to the sections for which they were responsible, the additions are not uniform throughout the text.[43]

Other changes result from Alfred's struggles with Gregory's elaborate Latin. Where the syntax of the Latin was involved, Alfred fre-

quently transformed Gregory's long periods into short sentences or clauses, sometimes expanding elements of the Latin in an attempt to clarify their meaning. For example, he translates a single phrase, *aqua more* (the properties of water) as a whole sentence ("But the human mind has the properties of water,"277), in this entire passage using thirty-four words to translate Gregory's fourteen.[44] Demonstrating a technique that would be used in subsequent translations, Alfred frequently translates a single Latin word with two words of English— *bellum* (war) becomes "battle and strife," for example, a change of primarily aesthetic rather than semantic value. The objective of his method of translation and paraphrase is aptly described by William H. Brown as "extracting the *sententia* and getting it down as clearly as possible."[45] It is not a method that aims primarily at revising or altering the significance of the source.

The *Pastoral Care* comprises four sections. Alfred follows Gregory's plan without significant departure and without extensive alteration. In order to differentiate the Old English from the Latin source, the speaker in the following summary will be identified as Alfred, who usually speaks in Gregory's voice. The first book enumerates the burdens on the bishop who occupies high pastoral office and the characteristics desirable in one who holds such office. The second describes how the good pastor should order his life, internally, or personally, and externally, or publicly. The third instructs the pastor to admonish and counsel his people, and tells him how to distinguish many classes of persons—rich and poor, mild and hot-tempered. The fourth and briefest book reminds the pastor of his own weaknesses.

The obligations of the pastoral life.   In Books 1 and 2 of the *Pastoral Care* each directive or admonition to the ruler carries with it a warning not to pursue any one objective without moderation. Appeals to action, and calls to accept leadership, are used to balance warnings that power must be exercised prudently and that corrupt or hypocritical motives may accompany the desire for power. This deliberative strategy mirrors Gregory's larger purpose, the reconciliation of active and contemplative lives; impulses to act are always to be checked by reflection on the consequences of action, but reflection is not allowed to become an excuse not to act. This strategy also creates the dialectical method of Gregory's argument, in which two alternatives are juxtaposed and the pastor is exhorted to avoid the extremes of either and to seek a middle ground.

The first section explains how the pastor should approach the position of power. The ruler must be learned, willing to live according to the wisdom he has acquired, and aware that power can corrupt and breed conceit which will make him unworthy of office. Warned that power will distract and preoccupy him, he is reminded that power must be used only for the benefit of others and not for reasons of vainglory. At the same time he should understand that he is not to avoid high office when divine decree calls him to it, for the desire to rule may be blameless. The section concludes with a brief description of the kind of man who is and who is not to rule.

The concept of the rightful use of power, introduced in Book 1, unifies the entire *Pastoral Care*; it is also the focus of Alfred's translation of Boethius's *Consolation of Philosophy*. The topic here dominates chapters 4, 5, and 6. Alfred approaches the right use of power through a discussion of teaching, which he pursues here, and elsewhere in Book 1, by adapting Gregory's inquiry to his own concern with education. Gregory wrote that "the government of souls is the art of arts" (a quotation he derived from St. Gregory Nazianzus); Alfred altered this to say that "teaching is the art of arts."[46] The substitution of "teaching" for "government of souls" signals Alfred's secularization of Gregory's spiritual mission and emphasizes the king's immediate, pragmatic concern with learning and leadership.

Gregory's preface warns against those who, although like him inexperienced in leadership, would nonetheless teach what they have not learned, appraising "the burden of authority the more lightly in proportion to their ignorance of its far-reaching responsibility."[47] Here again Alfred makes a purposeful substitution; Gregory's "burden of authority" becomes the "burden of teaching":

But there are many who are very similar to me in being unlearned, who, although they were never disciples, nevertheless wish to be teachers, and consider the burden of teaching very light because they do not know the power of its greatness. From the very door of this book—that is, from the beginning of this discourse—the foolish are driven away and reproached, who appropriate to themselves the art of teaching which they never learned. (24)

As would be expected of a king, Alfred defines the leader's role more sharply than his source. Indeed, he conflates the offices of king and teacher both in his translation of the text and in his preface. We see this conflation later in Book 1, when Alfred warns that the "care of teaching" sometimes distracts the ruler's mind (37). In Gregory's text rather than in Alfred's these cares are traced to government, not to teaching. Chief among the useless works that distract the ruler is vanity or self-importance. When Nebuchadnezzar extolled his own greatness, God transformed him into a beast as punishment, and the once-proud king suddenly became lower than all he had once ruled. "However, although I say this now," warns Alfred, "I do not censure great works nor legitimate power, but I blame a man for being proud because of them" (41).

Alfred explicates the concept of power righteously used more fully in the following chapter (5), which concerns teaching with example by using one's virtues. Here Alfred sets forth the strongest argument for taking power: by doing so one is useful to others and places one's self-concern in the background. Those endowed with great gifts are most fit to rule; if they spend time in contemplation, Alfred declares, they act immorally and are guilty of as many faults as they would have corrected had they been willing to work rather than contemplate (45). The ultimate example of such call to duty Alfred finds in Christ, who "came forth from the bosom of His father into our presence that He might help us" (47). The ruler who hesitates to exercise authority because he believes it will raise him above others unlawfully should, Alfred says, understand that true humility lies in following God's will. "When he is raised up and appointed so that he may be useful to others in the position which is offered him, he should shun it in spirit, and yet obediently accept it" (47).

Following Gregory, Alfred stresses self-knowledge and self-examination as requisites to leadership. "If he has not rejected his own vices," asks Alfred, "how can he cure the minds of other men, while he bears in his own mind many open wounds?" (59). He illustrates his point with the medical metaphor, perhaps more popular than any other in the text, which links physical illness and deformity to moral depravity, and compares the cure of sickness to contrition, confession, and penance.[48] As a physician, the pastor must be free of sickness before he can cure others. The most elaborate example of the metaphor illustrates the character of a man who should not rule. Quoting Leviticus 21:17–20, Gregory describes the unworthy ruler:

Concerning the heavenly voice which commanded Moses to tell Aaron that no man of their kin or household should offer any bread to his God, or come to his ministry, if he had any blemish: if he were blind or lame, if he had too large a nose, or one too small, or a crooked one, or if he had broken hands or feet, or if he were hump-backed, or bleary-eyed, or had flesh on his eye [a cataract], or a running sore, or ringworm, or hydrocele. (63)

Each physical flaw represents a moral defect: the blindness, ignorance of the light of divine contemplation; the little nose, inability to distinguish or discern; a great nose, immoderate subtlety in making distinctions; ringworm, a covetous mind which corrupts the body, and so forth. The defects together reflect the moral state of one so heavily afflicted: one subject to all these vices is unworthy to offer bread to God and cannot wash away the sins of others if he is ravaged by his own (73). Therefore, if the ruler himself is morally unfit, he can neither serve as an example of virtue nor superintend the moral lives of others.

The life of the pastor.   The second section of the *Pastoral Care* specifies how the pastor should conduct himself when he has attained holy office and enumerates ten qualities that the bishop must exemplify. In his works the bishop must surpass all others and remain pure of heart so that he can judge others fairly. He must also be exemplary in conduct, for he must both propose and demonstrate ideals, and he must be discreet, solicitous, and compassionate. He must strive to balance outward authority with inner humility, to rule out of love of God rather than vainglory, and to be cautious in distinguishing vice from virtue and in reproving those who do wrong. Finally, the ruler must be a reader who meditates on the holy law.

Several chapters focus on the ruler's need to be compassionate with those he rules, to be one with his people and yet be able to rise above them in contemplation as their intercessor. He should serve as an intermediary between his people and God. The teacher must sympathize with, and not despise, the weaknesses of others. He must link the highest with the lowest, mediating these extremes as Paul mediated the divine and the human through his apocryphal vision,[49] as Jacob ascended and descended his ladder, and as Moses went in and out of the temple. The priest too must link heaven with the cares of earth. The pastor ascends through contemplation, aspiring to the highest level without forgetting that his purpose in seeking the heights is to help those beneath him. "Because when love descends through mercy and attends to the needs of his neighbors, it rises wonderfully, and the more graciously it descends, the easier it ascends" (103).

Warned that he must put himself on the level of those in his charge, the priest is also commanded to recognize the essential inequality of men (chapter 17). All men are born alike, Alfred writes, but "some are kept behind others by the difference in their merits,

and their sins hold them there" (107).[50] Those with greater merit—
and less sin—are naturally set above the others. Yet they are not to
become proud because of their superiority. Even as he shows his outward authority, the ruler must not cease to be humble and to govern
through love, not fear. Qualifying this advice still further, Alfred
warns that fear is nonetheless an important part of social order and
that the ruler's subjects should fear him, "lest the power of governance be weakened" (119). But, in reproving his people, he cannot
be too severe, for fear may cause them to despair. The ruler must remain aware of his flock's weaknesses and must bind his people's sins
with instruction (123); his rule should combine severity and humanity.

Alfred uses sin as a means to distinguish rulers from the ruled. He
notes that Christ sometimes "spoke as if He did not know that He
was exalted above His brothers," saying, "We are become as little
children among you." However, when Christ saw sins to be punished, He spoke as master and lord. Seeking a rationale for worldly
authority in spiritual authority, Alfred and other rulers understood
Gregory's claim that "that kingdom is well governed, when he who
rules wishes rather to rule over the sins of men than over good men"
(117). Archbishop Hincmar of Reims, Alfred's contemporary, "agreed
with Gregory the Great that God had established kingship to deal
with the inequality in man brought about by his sin." Alfred too
would have believed that the king was God's deputy, who, because
he judged in God's stead, commanded the obedience of his people.[51]

The ruler's ability to mediate high moral standards and his peoples'
weaknesses depended on the pastor's chief office, the forgiveness of
sins. Confession and penance are referred to throughout the *Pastoral
Care*, but the system of private confession and penance, which Alfred
would have known, is not named. In Gregory's time the system of
penance was largely public rather than private. However, the Pope's
references to penance are general and theoretical, rather than practical
and liturgical, so that Alfred would have easily understood them as
applying to the private penitential system of his own day.[52]

The pastor is told to balance fear with love; his subjects should
never be so afraid of him or his power that they fail to confess (103);
rather, they should take refuge in him as a child would in its mother
and purify their sins with his help. At the same time, if a pastor is
too lenient in punishing sin, his charges will not learn to hate their
sins and will not accept punishment for them in this world, and so

will have to suffer more severely in the next (117). Alfred also reminds the pastor that he is often assailed with the same temptations as those who confess to him (105); because all men are subject to the temptations of the flesh, the confessor must remember his humanity, and consider "from his own circumstances how he will judge others" (159). How sinners are to be judged with fairness is the theme of Book 3. Book 2 concludes by advising the pastor to contemplate law and Scripture every day; if he does so, he can escape "his former love of bad habits," to which earthly companionship draws him, and can be "inspired and renewed for the heavenly regions" (169).

How the ruler should teach his subjects. The third section of the *Pastoral Care* enlarges on the priest's need for discretion in judging sinners; it is entirely devoted to describing different categories of men so that they can be taught, or "admonished," effectively. Each of the nearly forty chapters of Book 3 describes a class of people and advises the pastor how to approach and to teach that class. The scope of this section is immense; classes are determined according to age, material well-being, mental attitudes, personality traits, and almost every other conceivable aspect of the human condition. The practical value of Book 3 caused the *Regula* to be revered in the Middle Ages as a rhetorical handbook and a preaching manual.[53] According to Henry Davis, "It is this part of the work which commends it to succeeding generations, and still serves as a source of knowledge, inspiration, and enlightenment to rulers, pastors in high office or law, preachers, and confessors."[54]

Some categories are described only briefly, especially those concerning physical or material characteristics. The first chapter, for example, "That men are to be admonished in one way, in another women," merely says,

Men are to be taught more seriously and severely, and women more lightly; that the men may seek a greater burden, and the women be encouraged with flattery. (179)

Other brief distinctions are those between the young and the old, the sad and the glad, and masters and servants.

Many categories allow Alfred, following Gregory, the opportunity to expound at length, for the sake of instruction, on various aspects of human behavior. These sections require the pastor to exercise even-handed judgment and fairness. Book 3 again utilizes the balanced approach seen in Books 1 and 2, the coupling of encouragement with caution in the interest of avoiding extremes. Each chapter distinguishes two types of people. In the first part the merits of one type are set off against the flaws of the other; the conditions are then reversed to expose the weaknesses of the former and the strengths of the latter. Three chapters exemplify the method of this section; they concern rulers and subjects, sexuality, and sorrow for sin.

Discussing how rulers are to be judged by one standard and the ruled by another, Alfred observes that the ruled are not to be oppressed and that rulers are not to become intoxicated with their importance. Rulers set a good or evil example by their actions; if they mislead others, they shall be worthy of as many punishments as those they lead astray, "unless they afterwards cease, and convert as many as they can" (191). The ruler is not to close his eyes to the vices of his subjects, but to reprove them and correct them. Indeed, rulers should have eyes both outside and inside, "that they may satisfy the inner Judge in their own thoughts" as well as observe the weaknesses of their charges (195).

The ruled, too, are advised never to subvert or be disrespectful to their superiors. Gregory relates the story of Saul, who had persecuted David and forced him into hiding in a cave (1 Kings 24:6). On a journey, Saul unknowingly used this same cave to relieve himself. As he did so, David's men urged him to kill King Saul. Instead, David cut off part of the king's garment, thus forbearing to slay the king but, at the same time, reproving him for his injustice. In the story, David typified the good servant and Saul the unjust ruler: David blamed his lord, but secretly; later he repented for his disrespect. The story shows that rulers should not be criticized, "for when we offend against our lords" (even by criticizing them secretly) "we offend against the God who created authority" (201). This stands as one of the most uncompromising statements about authority in medieval literature: one who murmurs against his master murmurs against God. The merit of the point could not have been lost on Alfred, Hincmar, or other rulers who found in Gregory's text a guide to effective government.

Alfred adopts Gregory's attitudes toward sex and sexuality, already implied in the brief treatment of the difference between the sexes mentioned above, and he conveys the traditional medieval hostility toward sexual intercourse and sexual pleasure. Quoting Paul, Alfred writes, "Let those who have wives be as if they had none," explaining that "he has a wife as if he had none, who has her for physical pleasure, and yet on account of pleasure and love does not turn from better works" (395; 1 Corinthians 7:29). The married are to tolerate each other, to pray for each other's salvation, and to restrict sex to procreation. Those who must have sexual intercourse are saved, although they fall, provided that they fall "on the soft bed of marriage, not on the hard earth of fornication." Prayers may counteract the pleasure taken in intercourse. Married couples should remember that Paul permitted sex but did not command it, and spoke of it as if it were a sin. Those who cannot preserve continence should marry, Alfred concludes, again quoting Paul, "for it is written that it is better to marry than to burn" (401).

In the following chapter Alfred explains that virgins are to be admonished differently from the sexually experienced. He warns the latter that their salvation will be accomplished with great difficulty, while those who abjure sex will earn heaven by their sacrifice. But the pure are also warned that their purity, because it elevates them, makes them easier targets for temptation. If they withstand the assault of the world, like the eunuchs mentioned in Isaiah 56:4, they will have "cut away from themselves unrighteous works" and will inherit "eternal mansions in the Father's house ahead of his own children" (409). Those guilty of sins of the flesh should not despair, however. Often those inflamed with repentance after their acts are, because of their contrition, dearer to God than those who do not repent because they believe themselves to be free of sin. The contrite sinner gives God greater happiness than the ninety-nine righteous who do not repent (411).

The concluding section of Book 3 specifically addresses the pastor as preacher. The teacher should never forget, as he delivers instruction suitable to all men, that each must be instructed singly, since vices are individual. The teacher's correction should not be so strong as to overwhelm the patient, nor so mild as to leave the sinner unmoved. The teacher should be careful not to approach weak minds with difficult truths or to expose divine secrets to foolish men. The cock, a standard medieval figure for the preacher, should crow most loudly in the darkness of ignorance, and more softly as the light of learning nears (461). Elaborating on the metaphor, Alfred asks that the preacher should first arouse himself, as the rooster beats his wings before he crows, and then call others to good works. The teacher should remember that his works teach as loudly as his words; having called others with words, he should also summon them with his own good works (461). He must punish his own evils before calling attention to the sins of others, and he must display in his own actions the good qualities he will urge in others. These comments, which recall earlier discussions of leadership, conclude the third section of the *Pastoral Care*.

How the preacher should reflect on himself. The final section of the text, a single chapter, warns the teacher that he is not to become infatuated with his own eloquence, a point at which Alfred and Gregory appropriately draw their discussions to a close. In order to avoid such infatuation the teacher must contemplate his own infirmity, concentrate on what he has not yet done, and realize that sins remain—perhaps only small ones—which he has yet to amend. Alfred addresses his audience directly, admonishing the teacher to remember, "though you traverse the highest, that you are man," and to "consider very carefully the bridle of your infirmity, although you are raised above your condition" (467). In the final paragraph Alfred returns to Gregory's opening statement that he has tried to paint the portrait of the "ideal" pastor. Alfred, like Gregory, asks for a "plank of prayers in the shipwreck of this present life," and asks his friend to extend a hand to raise him, "for the burden of my own sins has oppressed me" (467). In his conclusion Alfred appropriately illustrates many of the principles of humility, repentance, and self-examination outlined in the *Pastoral Care*, exemplifying thus the virtues he has encouraged.

Alfred's translation of the *Regula Pastoralis* concludes with a verse epilogue, found in only two manuscripts, including the oldest, Oxford, Bodleian Library, Hatton 20.[55] The ornate style of the epilogue resembles Alfred's richly figurative preface to his translation of the *Soliloquies* of Augustine.[56] According to the epilogue, water, a metaphor for wisdom from the Holy Spirit, flows through books into the minds of men; some retain it, and others let it flow aimlessly in "shallow streams over the fields." The wise man fills his vessel with this water and drinks deeply from it. A leaky vessel cannot hold the water and should be repaired quickly lest it cause one to lose "the drink of life." Neither the epilogue nor the metrical prologue to Alfred's translation has been adequately studied. Their vocabulary, their meter, and the ornate figures they employ all await investigation.

Critical History and Links to Other Translations

Alfred's *Pastoral Care* was more highly esteemed in his own day than in ours. The text was a favorite of the chief writers in the later

Old English period, Archbishop Wulfstan and the eminent homilist
Ælfric.[57] However, in recent times the artistic and literary merits of
the text have seldom been praised. The tone for modern criticism
was, perhaps, set by Henry Sweet in his edition of 1871. Then an
Oxford undergraduate, Sweet stated that the *Pastoral Care* was of "exclusively philological interest."[58] Sweet's low opinion of the text has
endured. C.L. Wrenn dismissed it as "uneven and often confused or
slavish, so that it has no literary merit."[59] Even more recent and sympathetic readers, including William H. Brown and Ingvar Carlson,
have bestowed few words of praise. Brown dismissed it as a "dreary
tract in Latin turned into a dreary tract in English," adding: "What
little we may like there, besides some skillful manipulation of the difficult syntax and diction, Alfred takes from Gregory. What we don't
have is enough of Alfred himself."[60]

Perhaps not surprisingly, much of what has been written about the
Pastoral Care concerns language. Indeed, one of the most intriguing
aspects of the *Pastoral Care* is the impact that study of the text has
had on Old English linguistic and literary scholarship. Prior to
Sweet's edition, scholars had treated the language of the tenth century
as "standard" Old English and had ignored the older West Saxon
forms preserved in the earliest manuscripts of this text. Sweet's introduction to the edition, an entertaining but highly partisan short
course in the history of Old English studies up to his time, attacked
the "irrational prejudices" of earlier editors with exceptional vigor.
Sweet was remarkably successful in establishing the importance of the
text and its linguistic forms but, unfortunately, contributed errors of
his own which until recently seem to have been overlooked.[61] Yet, by
providing the first description of the early West Saxon language,
Sweet opened a new area of studies in Old English. Indeed, scholars
now have difficulty imagining that the evidence he brought forth was
neglected so long.[62] Studies by Richard P. Wülker, Johann Ernst
Wülfing, and Gerhard Nickel draw upon examples from the *Pastoral
Care* to illustrate early Old English forms.[63]

The first attempts to analyze and characterize Alfred's style in the
Pastoral Care were two German dissertations; now more than a century old, they continue to serve as major sources on the topic of Alfred's alterations to Gregory's text.[64] More recent studies of Alfred's
style, drawing heavily upon examples from the *Pastoral Care*, include
works by Brown, which survey older scholarship and draw new conclusions about Alfred's techniques and purposes in translating, by

Carlson, by Ludwig Borinski, and by Paul Bacquet.[65] Unfortunately, most studies of the relation of Alfred's translation to its source fail to consider the development of different versions of Gregory's text, or to ask which version was used by Alfred. As a result, Alfred's translation is compared to a Latin text certainly at some remove from Alfred's source.[66]

Pending the establishment of the Latin manuscript tradition from which Alfred's translation descended, critical commentary on the *Pastoral Care* must focus on the relationship of this translation to other texts written by Alfred and his helpers. Anyone interested will soon discover, in spite of the critics' prejudices, that the *Pastoral Care* is rich in insights into medieval psychology and concepts concerning the right use of power and authority. Even though ideas are not, in this translation, subject to the kinds of expansion and interpolation that characterize Alfred's work as a translator elsewhere, the *Pastoral Care* represents our first evidence of his close acquaintance with several important images and themes.

Numerous figures found in the *Pastoral Care* reappear in later translations. In his *Soliloquies* Alfred will repeat images of trees that must be felled before a new building can be constructed. In the *Soliloquies* the trees represent ideas from which new buildings arise; in the *Pastoral Care* the image has a strictly moral application: the trees represent the wicked who must be reproved before they can become righteous, just as tall trees in the forest must be cut and allowed to dry before they can be used in building (442–44). Another metaphor frequent in the *Pastoral Care* and in the *Soliloquies* concerns vision as a figure for knowledge (chapters 1 and 46, among others).

In both the *Soliloquies* and the *Consolation of Philosophy* Alfred will compare the mind to a ship and, as in the *Pastoral Care*, will stress that unless the ship is anchored firmly, it will be borne away with the current and lost (444). The *Pastoral Care* also introduces the idea that evildoers are bestial (109), an important concept in the *Consolation*; the *Pastoral Care* also tells the parable of Lazarus and Dives (309), to which Alfred will return both in the conclusion of the *Soliloquies* and in his translation of the first fifty psalms. He added the Lazarus parable and anchor imagery to the *Soliloquies*; both figures might have been suggested to him or to his source by Gregory. Such additions provide us with an important index to Alfred's thoughts and, when taken together, help us to understand how he altered and enriched his Latin sources as he translated them.

The thematic links between the *Pastoral Care* and other translations are more important than common imagery. One theme which appears in later works is the need to reflect and to contemplate. At the conclusion to Book 2 Alfred states that contemplation makes the ruler a better teacher. "Be ready to teach," wrote Alfred, "and indulge every one who asks you rightly about the hope you have in you" (173). The need to contemplate also appears in Alfred's *Soliloquies*, again colored with regret at the king's inability to escape from worldly cares and restore peace of mind. We are reminded of Alfred's remark, reported by Asser, that among the things the king most desired and enjoyed too rarely, none was more important than solitude and time to contemplate.[67]

The major theme of the *Pastoral Care*, the proper use of power, anticipates Alfred's translations of both the *Consolation of Philosophy* and of the *Soliloquies*. In the *Pastoral Care* he worked within the framework of Gregory's concepts, which, as we have seen, were an important source of political theory in the early Middle Ages. In the translations of Boethius and Augustine, which were to come later in his career, Alfred explored his own ideas about the moral obligations of political power. His later discussions of the right uses of power would seem to derive from his early acquaintance with the concept in the *Pastoral Care*; however, scholarship rarely acknowledges this indebtedness.

The *Pastoral Care* deserves critical reassessment. Scholars such as Brown criticize the translation because it lacks originality in its departures from its source. But we cannot reasonably consider the *Pastoral Care* to be a lesser achievement merely because it transmits Gregory's teaching in a direct and straightforward manner. To do so is to judge Alfred by a standard of originality foreign to his time, to misinterpret the objectives of his program of educational renewal, and to devalue the elements in Gregory's work that appealed to him. The virtues of the *Pastoral Care* are easily identified. Informative, comprehensive, and authoritative, it was a wholly appropriate beginning to Alfred's program of translations. No other text of Alfred's period, and perhaps of the Middle Ages in general, could have spoken more clearly to the needs of an enlightened king in search of a means of educating, motivating, and redirecting his followers.

Chapter Four

The *Consolation of Philosophy:* Translation of Boethius

"No philosopher was so bone of the bone and flesh of the flesh of Middle-Age writers as Boethius. Take up what writer you will, and you find not only the sentiments, but the very words of the distinguished old Roman." So wrote Richard Morris in his edition of Chaucer's translation of the *De Consolatione Philosophiae.*[1] The immense popularity of Boethius in the Middle Ages is attested by the wealth of manuscripts of the *Consolation* in particular; recent estimates—still incomplete—number the copies at over four hundred.[2]

The *De Consolatione Philosophiae* is written in alternating prose and verse passages, a form called the *satura* or medley; the work encompasses several literary modes, including allegory, dialogue, dream vision, and, of course, the consolation, a work written to one in adversity, which seeks to reconcile him to his hardship. As an anthology of literary genres, the *Consolation* had considerable influence on medieval thought and letters, but not in the form Boethius gave to it. Instead, later writers adapted the *Consolation* through the "application, piecemeal and out of context, of thoughts, images and elegant phrasing which gave added point" to their own texts.[3] King Alfred was the first to translate the entire text into the vernacular.

The Manuscript Tradition

Little is known about the history of the *De Consolatione Philosophiae* in the centuries after Boethius's death, in 524, but an English scholar played a central role in introducing the text to the early Middle Ages. The Northumbrian Alcuin (d. 804) seems to have been the first to circulate the text; the leading scholar in Charlemagne's empire, he quoted from the *De Consolatione* frequently. Where Alcuin became acquainted with the text is not certain, but he probably encountered it at a continental school rather than in England.[4] Alcuin may have introduced the text to his homeland, but no firm evidence points to knowledge of the work in England before Alfred translated it.[5]

Unlike the original text, Alfred's version has a modest manuscript history.[6] Two complete copies and one fragment survive. The eldest (London, British Library, Cotton Otho A.vi), from the mid-tenth century, was badly damaged by fire in 1731; the other (Oxford, Bodleian Library, Bodley 180) dates from the first half of the twelfth century. Fortunately, variants from the Cotton manuscript were recorded before the Cotton library fire by Francis Junius, the seventeenth-century Dutch scholar, when he transcribed the Bodleian manuscript. Therefore, certain portions of the London manuscript, now illegible because of heat and water damage, can be reliably restored. A fragment of a third manuscript, a single leaf from the second half of the tenth century, was discovered in 1887 but has since disappeared.[7]

The manuscripts present Alfred's translation at slightly different stages of composition; neither complete manuscript records the work in its final form. The preface accompanying the Bodley version—wherein the text is divided into forty-two chapters—claims that Alfred first translated the text into prose and later versified portions that corresponded to the Latin meters. This manuscript, however, translates the meters in prose only. In the Cotton manuscript the Latin meters are translated into alliterating verses, which alternate with prose passages. But this manuscript does not include the preface, which must have been composed after the prose translation of the meters had been versified, and it does not divide the text into chapters.[8] The evidence of the preface suggests that stages of composition between those preserved in the extant manuscripts have been lost and that the tradition was considerably richer than its remnants.

The influence of Alfred's translation on other texts does not appear to have been great. Scholars periodically assert the debt of the Old English poem *Deor* to Alfred's text, but these arguments are not wholly convincing.[9] However, a century after Alfred's death the homilist Ælfric used the work, and we may assume that others did also.[10] And, like his *Soliloquies*, Alfred's *Consolation* survives in a manuscript from the twelfth century, suggesting that the difficulty of understanding the language of the ninth century in subsequent periods did not prevent later authors from appreciating the value of Alfred's translation. The Old English must have been even more difficult to read in the early fourteenth century, when Nicholas Trevet used Alfred's translation.[11] In Trevet's time the Latin text was known to En-

glish authors chiefly through French commentaries.[12] Not until
Chaucer was the *De Consolatione* again translated into English; thereafter, numerous translations, including one by Queen Elizabeth I, were
undertaken.[13]

Alfred's Authorship of the Translation

Few scholars have doubted that the Old English translation of the
Consolation of Philosophy is Alfred's. Evidence from early sources is un-
usually explicit. The *Chronicle* of Æthelweard, in the entry for 899
(the year of Alfred's death), comments that Alfred, an "unshakeable
pillar of the western people," was

a man replete with justice, vigorous in warfare, learned in speech, above all
instructed in divine learning. For he had translated unknown numbers of
books from rhetorical Latin speech into his own language—so variously and
so richly that [his] book of Boethius would arouse tearful emotions not only
in those familiar with it but even in those hearing it [for the first time].[14]

A manuscript that included Alfred's *Consolation* was among the
books given to Exeter Cathedral by Leofric, Bishop of Exeter (1046–
73).[15] William of Malmesbury twice speaks of Alfred's *Consolation*,
once to note that Asser assisted Alfred with it,[16] and again to comment patronizingly that such a translation, however necessary in Alfred's day, would have been "ridiculous"—that is, unnecessary—in
his own, more learned age.[17] The authorship of the versified meters
of the *Consolation* has been controversial; most scholars now agree that
Alfred was responsible for at least the prose meters found in the Cotton manuscript.[18]

The Latin Source: Boethius

The *De Consolatione Philosophiae* is a synthesis of ideas that Boethius
drew from many classical sources, including works of Greek and Roman philosophy and Latin poetry.[19] Writing in prison, he must have
consulted his sources only in memory, for he himself tells us that his
cell held few books.[20] The *Consolation* is a dialogue between Boethius
and Lady Philosophy, who appears to him in a dream. The work explores the nature of man's fortune and, in particular, seeks to explain
how the good can be permitted to languish in torment while the evil

prosper. Boethius never seeks to be freed from prison. Rather, he protests the order of a world in which evildoers prosper while those who struggle for justice and righteousness are falsely accused, convicted, and imprisoned.

The work consists of five books, in the course of which Lady Philosophy guides Boethius from despair to the realization that his imprisonment is part of the necessary order of the world and that, like all manifestations of fate or providence, it is purposeful. In Book 1 Lady Philosophy corrects the self-pity into which Boethius has fallen. She reminds him of his former high standing and agrees that his exile is cruel and unjust, but she reminds him that no one can drive him from his true homeland of wisdom but himself. Philosophy banishes the muses of poetry that Boethius has summoned; instead she offers the gentle, sweet remedies of her own wisdom. She warns that he has forgotten who he is: a mortal man subject to random chance in a world nevertheless purposefully guided by its Creator.

Book 2 is devoted to Philosophy's discussion of the true nature of fortune. Philosophy reminds Boethius that fortune's nature is to change—to favor man one moment and to abandon him the next—and tells him that human happiness cannot be complete. To believe that one is happy merely because one is favored by fortune is an illusion, she says, for happiness built on so weak a foundation cannot last. Boethius learns that just as good fortune traps man with the appearance of happiness in this life, bad fortune paradoxically frees him, revealing fortune for the fickle mistress she is, and putting the false delights of the goods of the world—material possessions, honor, and power—in perspective.

The longest and densest section of the *De Consolatione Philosophiae*, Book 3 amplifies and strengthens the "medicine" of Lady Philosophy's wisdom in Books 1 and 2. She instructs Boethius that all the good things man desires are merely fragments of the True Good; only when he embraces the True Good can man find perfect happiness. The supreme Good is the Creator, the source of all happiness, the only truly self-sufficient power. Because the Creator directs the universe, He directs all things toward himself, establishing the universal harmony that unites man and all creation.

In Book 4 Boethius asks Philosophy how, in a world governed by the Creator, evil not only can exist but can triumph. She replies that evil does not prevail, for God, who is all-powerful, desires only what is good. Therefore, evil men, whose desires contravene those of the

Creator, are powerless, for they can never attain the good that all good men desire. When Boethius complains that evil men nevertheless torment the just, Philosophy replies that the wicked are punished by their wickedness when it goes uncorrected, and that wickedness makes evil men unhappy. Finally, she declares that all fortune is good, for its purpose is either to reward the good or to punish the evil.

In the final book Boethius inquires about the role of chance in a world so closely and carefully governed. Philosophy replies that all events have causes, whether man perceives them or not. She stresses that divine providence, which manifests itself as chance, does not preclude man's free will (a point that would remain controversial throughout the Middle Ages); God knows how man will choose, but God's knowing does not determine man's choice. God sees all that was, is, and shall be as the eternal present: God knows all, as only He can, in an eternal, unchanging present. She concludes her address by urging Boethius always to act virtuously and to seek God's aid, for all that he does is done in the sight of this Judge. Thus, she tells Boethius, "Lift up your soul to worthy hopes, and offer humble prayers to heaven."[21] At the end of the *De Consolatione*, as Rand has remarked, we see that "deity is personal and prayer is a vital act."[22]

Alfred's Translation: An Overview of His Changes

While adhering to the general framework of the Latin text, Alfred substantially altered the thought and the design of the work. He knew Boethius through an augmented text which had acquired layers of commentary interpreting the classical elements of Boethius's world in a Christian context. Which commentaries in particular influenced his translation we do not know.[23] From among the many glossed manuscripts of the *Consolation* that survive, no single version accounts for all of Alfred's additions.[24]

Early commentaries originated on the Continent. One, written in the Loire valley in the mid-ninth century and subsequently brought to England, contains notes in Welsh handwriting dating from the ninth century; it has been associated with Bishop Asser, but it does not correspond closely to Alfred's version.[25] Asser also has been linked to another early commentary, but without firm proof.[26] Widely held assumptions about Alfred's exclusive dependence on commentaries have recently been challenged. In addition to commentaries, he may have borrowed selectively from various early medieval texts, such as the writings of Isidore of Seville, and the classics, including Vergil and other poets. Most similarities between the glosses and Alfred's version may be traceable to "shared traditions, coincidence, and a full consideration of context." This explanation seems plausible, for many ideas that Alfred added to Boethius are not found in the commentaries, while much that the extant commentaries add is not included by Alfred.[27]

Alfred directed a large-scale revision of Boethius's original. Some of the differences between his translation and the Latin are minor, but they form part of a comprehensive plan. Alfred explicated the names and places of Boethius's world for readers who would have been unfamiliar with them, additions which reflect the classical lore available to the king and his helpers.[28] For example, he explained that Mount Ætna is located in Sicily and that Bosiris was an Egyptian (chap. 16, 34, 36).[29] He also noted that seventy-two languages were spoken by different nations (chaps. 18 and 35).[30] Sometimes he transformed a passing allusion into a narrative. Alfred expanded a single sentence in the Latin about the giants' war on heaven; his description of a battle between the giants and Jove, prefaced by a denunciation of such "false stories," names the giants, tells the story of the Tower of Babel (again mentioning the seventy-two languages), and uses the giants' fall to exemplify the fate of all who "strive against the might of God" (Book 3, prose 12, chap. 35, 98). These additions sprang from Alfred's need to supply his audience with information it was not likely to possess, and his desire to moralize the historical episodes which in the original were sometimes merely passing allusions.

Alfred seems to have planted his text clearly in an ancient and partly mythological past. At the same time, he used the translation as a vehicle for his own commentaries on government and righteous living, thus giving it an idiosyncratic flavor and a relevance to his own world. Chief among the changes which stamp the text is Alfred's alteration of the names of the characters in his dialogue. First, he designated Boethius as "Mod," the Old English word for "Mind." He then changed the identity of "Mod," after Book 3, to "Boethius," and thereafter to "I." These changes may mark a steady progression away from the historical person of its Latin author to a speaker in Alfred's own time, the "voice" of Alfred himself, or the collective voice of Alfred and his assistants.

Alfred also changed the identity of Boethius's interrogator, Lady Philosophy, in some places calling her "Gesceadwisness" (meaning "reason" as well as "wisdom") and more often "Wisdom" (the word in Old English and in modern English). The change of Lady Philosophy's name has a counterpart in Alfred's translation of the *Soliloquies*, a dialogue between Reason and Augustine concerning the search for wisdom.[31] As a result of these changes in names, Alfred's *Consolation* becomes something that the Latin original was not—a dialogue between the mind (Mod) and Wisdom (or Reason), a power of the mind. Alfred's translation is not a lecture delivered by a wise figure who appears in a dream, but a debate between the Mind and its own faculties, the powers which can guide Mod to happiness.

Alfred's large-scale revision called for an overhaul of basic assumptions underlying the Latin as well as for the addition of explanatory detail. His theological concepts in particular, which appear to have motivated many of his changes, have either no exact or only a weak counterpart in the original. From the Neoplatonic speculation of Boethius, which is not overtly theological (although hardly incompatible with Christianity), Alfred fashioned a thoroughly orthodox Christian treatise. His reflections on government, wealth, power, and fame differ sharply from the attitudes of Boethius. Alfred consistently viewed these earthly preoccupations more positively, and gave more emphasis to them in his arguments than did his source. He recast the Latin boldly and imaginatively but not quite coherently: even at its best his version cannot match the compressed elegance and clarity of the original text. A blend of philosophy, mythology, and theology, Alfred's *Consolation* represents his own thought at its richest and most diverse, and it exhibits a variety and vitality not easily recaptured in paraphrase. The following summary preserves the outline of Alfred's original, indicating the chapter divisions of the Old English as they correspond to the five books of Boethius.

Alfred's Translation

Book 1, chapters 1–6. Alfred began his translation with a historical prologue which has no counterpart in the Latin. The prologue sketches the Goths' conquest of Rome, Theodoric's reign, his belief in Arianism (a heresy asserting that Christ was not divine but merely the best of mortal beings), his "countless crimes," including the murder of the Pope, and Boethius's part in the conspiracy to rid the empire of the tyrant. This material is expanded in the metrical version of the prologue, which recounts the arrival of the Gothic troops in Italy.[32] The prologue strikingly alters the circumstances of Boethius's imprisonment. In the original Boethius's misfortune did not result from his own misdeeds. But Alfred states that Boethius actually did plot to overthrow Theodoric, and thus was not, as is widely believed, falsely accused by the emperor. Mod is the agent of his own downfall, rather than the victim of caprice and conspiracy. Unlike his Latin counterpart, he is guilty of treason, and his guilt compromises his outrage at being punished. Although Mod insists that he suffers because he defended justice and honor, he is forced to accept responsibility for his fall, and for restoring himself to happiness and peace of mind.

By altering the circumstances of Boethius's imprisonment, Alfred was able to introduce a radically new theme central to his translation: man cannot merely resign himself to his fate, as the Latin text teaches, but must take responsibility for his ill fortune and find within himself the power to correct it. Alfred argues that man can determine his fate, not by controlling events outside his realm, but by directing his own will to the good and by performing good acts. Alfred thereby contradicts Boethius's central assumption about the mysterious nature of fate: for Alfred, God's ways may be unknown to man, but they are not mysterious manifestations of a plan beyond man's comprehension.

The narrative mode of Alfred's translation alternates uneasily in the first chapter between first person and third person until the dialogue with Wisdom, reported in the third person, is established. When Book 1 opens, Boethius is prostrate with grief and weeping. Given that Boethius is, in Alfred's version, guilty of treason, his despondency may smack of self-pity, for he has not been imprisoned without cause. Suddenly, Wisdom appears. She banishes worldly cares from Boethius's mind and draws nearer his "grieving intellect," lifting it to her.

Looking at Wisdom, Mod recognizes his former teacher, who accuses him of forgetting what she has taught him and promises to show him his error. He asks if his present misery is the reward of one who has followed wisdom; does his life bear out Plato's maxim that without righteousness no power is righteous? (chap. 3.4, 9). With the severity that characterizes her throughout the work, Wisdom replies that he has caused his own downfall: no man departs from a righteous purpose unless he himself wishes to do so (chap. 5.1, 11). At the end of Book 1 she identifies Mod's two most important errors: he assumes that the evil govern the world, a view she will later challenge; and he believes that fate controls life independently of God's plan. He admits to this latter belief, and Wisdom, encouraged by his progress, promises to help him regain his happiness.

Book 2, chapters 7–21. In Book 2 Wisdom prepares Mod to redefine the sources of his happiness by exploring the falseness of happiness founded on worldly possessions and power. Alfred made major additions to his source in order to stress, first, that man is the agent of his own unhappiness and is not the victim of capricious fortune, and, second, that through the proper exercise of power man can acquire true and unchanging happiness.

Alfred assigned to Wisdom a speech that Boethius had assigned to Fortune. In the original Fortune scornfully explains how she disabuses man of his illusory happiness and brings the proud low. To change is her nature: spinning her wheel, she raises the low and lowers those on high (Book 2, prose 2). Alfred astutely omitted the wheel of fortune from his version, a change that allowed Wisdom to fix Mod with the blame for his downfall. In Alfred's translation Wisdom does not describe the random motion of fortune's wheel. Alfred transforms the revolving of the wheel into Wisdom's benevolent flight into the skies; with her servants, she encircles the heavens, raises the humble to heaven, and brings heavenly blessings to the lowly. She invites Mod to come aloft with her servants—knowledge and skill of various kinds, and true riches—on the condition that he afterwards return to earth to serve "the needs of good men" (chap. 7.3, 18).

Wisdom swiftly brings Mod to a realization that his errors have cost him his peace of mind. "But you were too confident in your righteousness and in your good purpose," she says, "thinking that no unrighteous thing could come upon you, and desiring to have the reward of all your good works in this world" (18). Mod sought reward for his good actions in worldly rather than spiritual comforts; when he lost the fame and material goods that constituted his reward, he also lost his fondness for them and began to understand their emptiness. Mod admits his error: "I understand that I am guilty on each count, and am so overwhelmed with sorrow for the offense that I cannot answer you" (chap. 8, 19). Wisdom urges him to be ashamed rather than despondent, for "he who is ashamed is on the way to repentance" (20). From this position, Mod's lowest point, Wisdom now begins to lift him.

She does so by reminding Mod that even in the utter despair of his fallen state he has not lost all of his happiness. He still has his family—his wife, two fine sons, and his wife's father. The social cohesion formed by kinship and friendship is one of the rewards that fortune cannot take from him. Alfred describes these kinsmen as anchors that keep Mod from complete desolation in this life; these anchors have a counterpart in the life to come, the triad of virtues: faith, hope, and love.[33]

Kin and friends are one resource through which Mod can find happiness, but he notes that these anchors are not "fast and enduring" (chap. 10, 23). The foundations of his vanished happiness, the rewards of fortune, have disappeared and left him miserable; unlike those rewards, the happiness that lies within cannot be lost (chap. 11.2, 25). In the following chapter Alfred's Wisdom returns to the charge of covetousness leveled against Mod at the beginning of the *Consolation*. She criticizes Mod's excessive love of that which is beneath him—worldly goods—and chastises his weak love of himself and of the Lord who made him. When Mod replies that loving the beautiful things of the world cannot be wrong, Wisdom rejoins that their beauty is not man's. He should desire to possess only what he naturally needs: not the riches sought by the unrighteous and intemperate, but "meat and drink and clothes, and tools with which to exercise the skills you have and that are natural to you, and that may be rightly used" (chap. 14.1, 30).

Alfred added this list of the things necessary to man's existence in the world; it is one of his most telling changes, for in it Wisdom explains how man, fallen into unhappiness through his own covetousness, through abuse of the world's goods, can find true happiness by using the world's resources properly. Alfred argues, against his source, for moderation in the use of worldly goods and gifts rather than for rejection of them. He does not praise gold, but rather skills, tools, and the materials necessary to productive living. These goods are natural to man, for they serve his talents and enable him to act virtuously. But Wisdom denounces the desire for excessive wealth and riches as greed. She warns Mod to value only those riches that lie within him, the three elements of the Divine which liken him to his

Creator: his reason, his memory, and his will (chap. 14.2, 32). Although he undervalues them and fails to use them, they cannot be taken from him.

Wisdom then commemorates the "Golden Age," when all men took only what they needed from the earth, followed the laws of nature, and were not covetous. That age ended when evil men began to fight over the world's wealth and all peace in the world was lost (chap. 15, 33–34). Wisdom's paean to the lost glories of the perfect world is followed by a stinging denunciation of worldly power. She thereby introduces the concept of power around which Alfred organized many of his changes in this section of the *Consolation*. She shows Mod that power often comes to the most unworthy men, and fails to make them worthy. Theodoric, Boethius's captor, is used to illustrate her claim that "power is never good, unless he is good who has it." She adds that "no man acquires skill and excellence because of his power, but instead he acquires power because of his skill and his excellence. No man is the better because of his power; if he is good, it is because of his skill" (chap. 16.1, 35). In other words, power is not in and of itself good or evil: it derives its moral quality from the man who applies it. Wisdom commands Mod to "study wisdom" because wisdom is the secret of happiness and the source of power: "If you are wise and good, power will follow you, even though you do not desire it" (35).

In his response Mod appropriates Wisdom's own exhortation about tools and applies her concept of skill. He defends his conduct and justifies his pursuit of earthly power. Mod insists that he never took delight in either covetousness or power, claiming only that he "wanted tools and materials to do the work I was commanded to do, which was that I should virtuously and suitably guide and wield the power that was entrusted to me" (chap. 17, 40).

Mod argues that no one can develop his natural gifts or govern without the necessary materials and tools. Merging his voice with that of Alfred, Mod lists the materials that a king needs to govern: a well-peopled land, men of prayer, men of war, and men of work; he also needs land to dwell in, gifts, weapons, meat, ale, clothing, and whatever else the three classes of men need (40).[34] But he adds that wisdom is essential to the proper use of skills; without wisdom, one's skills cannot be fully developed and will soon be forgotten. Mod desires material goods so that he may govern well and use his special talents. But he wishes to use his skills wisely so that he may live honorably in this life and live on through the memory of his good works after his death (41).

Mod has joined the right use of power and possessions to the possession of wisdom. In Mod's speech, Alfred's addition, the king brilliantly reaffirmed Lady Philosophy's denunciation of the abuse of power while justifying his own enlightened approach to it. However, Wisdom discourages Mod from the pursuit of fame, claiming that the desire for fame makes men yearn for unrighteous power and distorts their reason and judgment (chap. 18.4, 45). To prove that earthly fame is worthless, Wisdom reminds Mod that many great men have died and been forgotten. No one remembers even Weland, a famous goldsmith, even though he was wise.[35] "I say that he was wise," she adds, "because the wise man can never lose his skill, and it cannot be taken from him any more than the sun can turn from its station" (chap. 19, 46). In her rebuttal Wisdom asserts that skill confers wisdom: skill is worth having and worth cultivating because, unlike fame, it cannot be taken away.

Wisdom does not criticize Mod's desire for skills wisely used, but she harshly denounces his desire for fame, which she portrays as a hollow and inconsequential prize. Seen from the perspective of the heavens, earth and all its honors, including fame, dwindle to insignificance. Having succeeded in convincing Mod that earth's rewards are trivial and that the loss of them, which at first seems to be a calamitous adversity, is not to be lamented, Wisdom now turns Mod's attention to the unexpected benefits of bad fortune. Wisdom wishes to separate Mod from the sources of false happiness. She claims that adverse fortune is more useful than good because it helps man distinguish friend from foe. In Boethius's original Lady Philosophy praises the ability to distinguish true from false friends because friends are "the most precious kind of wealth" (Book 2, prose 8); in the metrical section which follows, Lady Philosophy praises the love that "joins people together by a sacred bond" and rules the heavens in perfect order (Book 2, poem 8).

Following his source, Alfred analyzes friendship in the context of a statement about the power of love to create universal harmony (chap. 21). But he vastly increases the importance of friendship as a force creating social harmony. Lady Philosophy's poem, probably the most famous of all the meters in the *Consolation*, is the "classic statement of the medieval idea that love is the principle of harmony in the universe."[36] Recasting his source, Alfred translates the "love" praised by Lady Philosophy as "God" who "has so caught and led, and managed all his creatures with his bridle, that they can neither be still nor move more swiftly than He allows them with his rein" (chap. 21, 49). Just as God holds the conflicting elements of the world in harmony, He unites all creatures in friendship: "He gathers friends and companions so that they hold their kinship and their friendship truly" (50). Thus to be able to tell one's false friends from those who are faithful creates more than peace of mind: it creates security in one's community. Alfred's attention to the theme of friendship, which sometimes distorts the arguments of his source, reflects his concern for the security and the loyalty of his followers. For Alfred, friendship is not only "the most precious kind of wealth," as Boethius said. The foundation of social cohesion and community, friendship creates order and harmony in the world: it is Alfred's vision of love and, simultaneously, a subtle means of discouraging political resistance.

Book 3, chapters 22–35. Book 3 repeats and expands Wisdom's earlier definitions of true and false happiness. Some men define the true good as riches, honor, sovereign power, fame, merriment, power to amass wealth, and wives. But Wisdom dismisses all these allurements and declares the most precious of all happinesses to be "True Friendship" (chap. 24.3, 54). Other things of the world are sought because they bring power or pleasure, but eventually they divide men, create foes, and fail to satisfy. Friendship alone brings harmony. In the Latin Lady Philosophy does not construct a comparable defense of friendship, but declares that friendship is of two kinds— one desired because it is virtuous, the other desired because it promises power or pleasure—and that the venal kind is more common. She implies that friendship sought because it brings power is, like the desire for riches or fame, only false happiness to be despised.

Alfred's translation departs from Lady Philosophy's argument to assert, first, that friendship is created not by fate but by God, and, second, that friendship is a natural and inseparable union of men (54). While other kinds of happiness ultimately fail man and leave him seeking satisfaction, true friendship will not desert him. Alfred's comments on friendship in Book 3 must be understood in the light of his definition of friendship and kinship as sources of social harmony under God's governance in Book 2. There friendship is the force of love that holds the community together; Alfred could not permit Wisdom to dismiss as a reward of false fortune an institution he had understood and praised as God's means of creating social harmony.

In succeeding chapters Wisdom demonstrates the superficiality of the rewards of riches and power. The king who bestows wealth and power on his "darlings" is not really powerful, for he wishes to have even more than he already has: his wealth and power bring dread and sorrow, not happiness (chap. 29, 67). By asserting that no one who possesses power can be free of the fear of losing it, Wisdom reiterates her earlier claim that power does not make good the king who holds it, and that power and wealth do not bestow virtue on the king who pursues them. When the king's wealth departs, so do the friends who were loyal only because the king was wealthy and powerful. Only a few friends remain true, and they would have loved a friend even if he were poor. To be rid of false friends, then, is a hidden benefit of the adversity that deprives the king of his wealth, for nothing is worse than a foe in the likeness of a friend. Wisdom again reminds Mod that, except for the love of true friends, no earthly reward can be the source of power. All other rewards, such as wealth and power and false friends, will depart with good fortune. Those rewards breed fear and insecurity; they destabilize society and destroy harmony.

Wisdom now reaches her central lesson, that true power and happiness cannot be found in the rewards of the world, but only in strength of the soul. Power is self-sufficiency, freedom from external need, which the rich and famous can never know. Wisdom concludes her presentation of the "resemblances" of happiness by naming the source of true power, those things that man most wishes for: power, self-sufficiency, fame, honor, and good temper. United, these qualities are God: "When the five qualities are joined together . . . they make but one whole, and that whole is God" (chap. 33, 76). By dividing this unity into parts, as man necessarily must do with his "idle words" in this life, he finds neither God nor the Good. But, by exercising power over his mind, man can turn from earthly to higher rewards. Wisdom stresses that power over the mind is best achieved in prayer (chap. 33); in the prayer that follows, Wisdom praises the harmony of creation and God's power over all. Alfred's version of the prayer, the longest addition to his translation, greatly alters the famous hymn in which Boethius extols God's harmonious governance of the universe (Book 3, poem 9).

Having learned to define happiness as self-sufficiency, and having been told that power over his happiness is to be found only in the mind, Mod must now seek happiness. The mind can find within itself all the good it seeks from without, but teaching is needed to nurture the seed of truth which ever abides in the soul. Wisdom quotes Plato: "Whoever is unmindful of righteousness should turn himself to his memory; there he will find righteousness hid amid the sloth of the body and the distractions and afflictions of the mind" (chap. 35.1, 95).

To illustrate the power of the mind, Wisdom tells Mod one of the favorite stories of the Middle Ages, that of Orpheus and Eurydice. The legend supports Alfred's themes by stressing both the opportunity to choose between good and evil and the second chance that repentance offers to those who have chosen incorrectly. Mourning his dead wife, Orpheus charmed all of hell with his music. Moved to pity, the judge of souls granted him the return of Eurydice on condition that she follow him out of hell and that he not look back at her until they had left hell. But, as the couple neared the border, Orpheus turned and thus lost Eurydice forever.

As Boethius construed the legend, Orpheus disobeys by looking away from goodness. Alfred's Orpheus, however, is more than a lawless lover; he errs in a specifically Christian context by rejecting the light of "True Goodness," God. And, looking instead on his old sins, Orpheus takes a step toward committing them again. In Alfred's version Eurydice stands not for the pit of hell or, more acceptably, for the attractions of earth, but for the sins of one's past life. Alfred's Orpheus must choose not between the light of inner knowledge and the darkness of hell, but between seeking good and returning to evil. His mind does not turn to the darkness of error—philosophical confusion—but to sin. In Alfred's interpretation man can correct his failure to turn his eyes toward the good, and can repent his sins and save himself.

Book 4, chapters 36–40.5.   Book 4 discusses the most complex of the questions raised by earlier books of the *Consolation*, the apparent triumph of evil over good. Acknowledging that Wisdom's knowledge comes from God, Mod asks Wisdom why God allows evil to exist and to triumph over good (chap. 36). Mod's challenge forces Wisdom to clarify the definitions of power and true happiness which were developed in Book 3. (The reader of Alfred's translation would do well to refer to a good translation of the Latin at this point. Difficult philosophical issues are often explained more clearly and effectively in the Latin than in the Old English.)

Wisdom's claim that good men always have power and that evil men are never powerful rests on a central premise that all men desire true happiness—happiness that rises above the mutable goods of earth—and that true happiness is synonymous with goodness. Thus all men, whether good or evil, share a desire to be happy, to be good. Wicked men are frustrated in their search for goodness; should they find goodness, they would no longer be evil. Such men are ultimately powerless because they cannot achieve the goodness they desire. Even though they are capable of reason, they refuse to pursue virtue and wisdom; they are victims of sloth, unwilling to reform themselves, and of greed, blinding themselves by material rewards. Disabled by sloth and greed, evil men will not forswear vice; they continue to do evil only because they cannot do good. Thus Wisdom concludes that they have lost the existence proper to their nature. Wicked men have no "fellowship" in happiness and suffer for their evil purpose. Therefore, Mod need not lament the triumph of evil, for that triumph is not lasting: either in this life or the next, evildoers reap the rewards of their actions.

For the same reasons that evil men are weak, good men are strong. They both desire to do what is good and are able to do it. Because their desires for goodness are fulfilled rather than frustrated, they are powerful. Good men always accomplish what they wish, either by actualizing it or merely by intending it; both their intentions and their actions result in goodness. Thus Wisdom has contradicted Mod's claim that evil triumphs and that the good is everywhere subordinated to it.

Wisdom now recapitulates her complex arguments. She has defined power as the highest form of good, automatically eliminating those who do evil from the ranks of the powerful (chap. 36.8, 110). She has linked the desire for power to the desire to do good works: "Therefore the power that man may do good is ever to be desired, for that is the best power: that man wishes to do well, and is able to do so" (110). Even the intention to do good is rewarded if man is unable to bring his good intention to fruit in action. The desire to do good counts as heavily as the good that is performed; both the good works and the will to do them are rewarded in the next world (111).

Mod now understands that true happiness depends on the merits of good men, and unhappiness on the merits of the evil. Yet he also claims to be shocked at the punishments of wicked men that are imposed on those who are good (chap. 39, 124). He asks how the suffering of the good can be reconciled with Wisdom's claim for universal harmony and order; does not such suffering contradict Wisdom's claim that all happens in accord with God's will?

These questions reflect Alfred's struggle to transform Boethius's vision of universal harmony into one of a world governed with perfect justness by God. Wisdom distinguishes between Providence and Fate: Providence is "divine reason," God's knowledge of what will happen to us; Fate is the working of God's will in the world. Because Fate is subject to Providence, even random events manifest the will of God. In order to create an image of a perfectly ordered world, with God at its center, Alfred describes all creation as a wheel. The axle of the wheel represents God, the unchanging, unmoving center, outward from which, and along the wheel's spokes, are men. "The nave moves nearest the axle; therefore it moves more surely and more securely than the rim; so the axle may be the highest good, which we call God, and the best men travel nearest to God, as the nave rotates nearest to the axle." The farther men range from the axle, the greater their physical suffering and spiritual confusion (chap. 39.7, 129).[37] The greater one's distance from the center, the greater one's difficulty in seeing God and understanding the workings of the universe. Thus Wisdom claims that all things happen justly, even though Mod does not perceive them to happen in that way, and that man's dullness, not God's unrighteousness, is at fault when events do not turn out as man expects (chap. 39.9, 132).

Book 5, chapters 40.5–42. Mod asks how, in a world perfectly ordered by God, man can have freedom or the power to do as he wishes (chap. 40.7, 140). Recalling the image of the wheel, Wisdom replies that man's degree of freedom depends on his closeness to God. Angels are freer than men because they desire no wrong, while those men who are closest to earthly things and bow to vice have no freedom at all. But this scheme, which conforms to the wheel image described in Book 4, troubles Mod for two reasons: first, he wonders if divine foreknowledge contradicts the freedom that Wisdom claims for human will; second, he asks why God, who knows all that men intend, does not prevent the evil from acting unrighteously (chap. 41.1, 141).

Wisdom replies by asserting the freedom of human will. God has given man the will to do as he pleases, limiting his freedom only by death; he is not like a king who governs only slaves. (Wisdom claims that death can be postponed by good deeds; how this happens she does not explain [chap. 41.1, 142].) Pursuing his concern with the futility of life in a predetermined world, Mod asks if good works, such as prayer and almsgiving, have meaning if good men are ordained to goodness and cannot choose to be evil. If good works were not meaningful, Wisdom replies, the commandments to do good and to avoid evil would be in vain, and the concept that God rewards each according to his works would have no meaning (chap. 41.3, 144).

The philosophical ideas of Alfred's translation are sometimes difficult to separate from traditional Christian doctrine. Alfred's version of the *Consolation* asserts specific theological truths and alters the thought of Boethius to conform to them. While the universal harmony of Boethius is presided over by a remote, impersonal god, the God who stands behind and gives order to Alfred's world is a just, all-seeing judge who requites the evil and rewards the good. Alfred's translation closes with an exhortation to pray:

Lift up your hearts to Him when you raise your hands, and pray for what is right and needful for you, for He will not deny you. Hate evil, and flee from it as you best may do; love virtues and follow after them. You have great need that you do what is good, for what you do is ever done before the eternal and almighty God, who sees and requites all. (149)

Alfred calls upon his readers to act righteously and to believe in God. His version of the *Consolation* makes a sustained appeal to the pursuit of wisdom and righteous action. Alfred's *Consolation* reveals a pragmatic, practical bias, a concern with proper conduct in the world of politics and power. Key elements of the king's educational program are called to mind throughout the text: the need to teach men to understand the best thought and the obligation of leaders to exercise power in the light of moral teaching. For Alfred these concerns were not theoretical. He understood that the right use of power was based on virtue and could be realized in the material world. His revision of the *De Consolatione Philosophiae* bears vivid witness to his conviction that unless rulers are wise they cannot rule well.

Alfred's Meters of Boethius

The preceding summary has treated Alfred's translation of Boethius as a continuous prose document, acknowledging only some of its metrical sections. However, wishing to be faithful to his original, Alfred or his helpers retranslated into verse those prose passages that had been translated from the meters in his source. The literary quality of the meters remains insufficiently appreciated. Studies by Allan A. Metcalf and John W. Conlee acknowledge their merits.[38] Stanley B. Greenfield finds them "not especially noteworthy" but does not dismiss them;[39] C.L. Wrenn, however, regards the verse as little more than a paraphrase of the prose.[40] The meters may rank well below the best Old English poetry, but they have their merits.[41]

To compare the prose translation with the corresponding poetry, examining the many ways in which Alfred augmented and varied the verse, is a fruitful critical exercise.[42] Alfred and his helpers employed the devices of poetry to transform the prose, heightening and sharpening its effect. A case in point is the preface, which recounts Theodoric's conquest of Rome and stresses Boethius's plot to overthrow the emperor.[43] Expanding the prose, the verse describes the gradual progress of the Goths and their two kings, Alaric and Raedgod, through Italy to Rome. The poet first pictures the army as a distant and remote threat, and then confronts readers and Romans alike with the shields and banners of the attackers at the city's gates (11. 1–11). This episode, briefly passed over in the prose, affords an effective, if conventional, glimpse of Old English battle poetry. While the Old English *Consolation* may not equal the aesthetic elegance of the Latin original, the alternating pattern of prose and poetry is a beautiful reminder that Alfred himself saw the *Consolation* as part song.

Critical History

The critical reputation of Alfred's *Consolation of Philosophy* has always been high. Kurt Otten ranks it as "Alfred's most ambitious work and the finest achievement in the history of Old English prose."[44] Because Alfred's translation contains many ideas not in the original, some scholars question how accurately Alfred reflected his source and how successfully he set forth his own coherent philosophy. A few readers, seeking to excuse the translation's occasional lack of clarity, have doubted the capacity of the Old English philosophical vocabulary to express Boethius's sophisticated reasoning. They argue that Alfred's .translation both simplified and distorted the source.[45] However, a recent comparison of Alfred's philosophical language with that of Chaucer has refuted this claim. Alfred's English has been shown to be no less expressive of abstract concepts than the English of Chaucer.[46] Alfred may have generally eschewed complex argument—as a concession to his audience, some think—in favor of direct and commonplace analogies. But the limitations of his translation were imposed by the complexity of his subject and his own grasp of philosophy, not by the vernacular language he used.[47]

Critical discussions of the *Consolation* have tended to focus on Alfred's additions, their sources, their significance, and, especially, their autobiographical value. Some readers have detected traces of the king's own creed in his extensive departures from the Latin source, and have suggested parallels between the Latin author and Alfred. Wrenn, for example, believed that the text had "special appeal for Alfred," since his life, "beset by every difficulty—in ruling his kingdom as well as through his intense physical ailments (if Asser is to be believed)—had many parallels with that of the Roman statesman."[48] More plausibly, Malcolm Godden has suggested that Alfred's preface, which recounts the barbarian invasion of Rome, echoes his own concern with the recent Danish invasions of England.[49]

In a recent and widely admired work F. Anne Payne claims that Alfred and Boethius shared

the determination to create and build in the face of a civilization that was crumbling all around them. In their lives and in their major work, it is this trait that stands out more clearly than any other similarity; and it is their effort to find something permanent in the flux of decay that gives their works a relevance to ages beyond their own.[50]

However, the resemblances between the classical philosopher and the Anglo-Saxon king are easily exaggerated, and the obvious differences between them easily overlooked. Surely Alfred would have had no more in common with Boethius than with Augustine, Gregory, or many other Latin authors. To appreciate Alfred's translation of the *Consolation of Philosophy* does not require the assumption that Alfred fashioned his text in circumstances similar to those that surrounded Boethius. In fact, almost all readers of Boethius, most of whom have never been in prison, have found the plight of the noble Roman evocative of their own preoccupations and doubts about their happiness. The work's general appeal was and is so great that no special affinity between Alfred and its author needs to be stressed as Alfred's motive for choosing to translate it.

The biographical approach has led some readers to stress—indeed, to exaggerate—Alfred's originality and to minimize his debt to his sources, both to Latin commentaries on the *Consolation* and to other Christian and classical texts. Payne advances particularly ambitious claims for the text as Alfred's "own examination of the universe," claiming that he completely overhauled the text, substituting for the pervading Boethian concept of order his own concept of freedom.[51] But by rejecting the Boethian God and the perfectly ordered world emanating from Him, Alfred did not necessarily substitute for it another philosophical system, this one based on freedom rather than fate.

Payne asserts that Alfred's solution to the problem of freedom in a determined universe "has more similarities to those of the recent writers William James and Paul Tillich than to those of Boethius and St. Augustine."[52] But many scholars would be wary of suggesting that Alfred was not, in spite of all that we know about him, a man of his time and that he neither entertained a vision of eternity nor saw the natural world as a symbol of spiritual order. While allowing that "the dark Germanic vision" of a chaotic world occasionally intrudes on Alfred's thought, Katherine Proppe is foremost among those who argue for his adherence to concepts of eternal order and the conventional Christian perspective of his day.[53] Milton McC. Gatch, too, argues that Alfred's belief in Christian doctrine is not overwhelmed by the impact of *wyrd*, the Germanic concept of fate, on Alfred's worldview. Rather, Alfred sees "Providence controlling events in accordance with the dictates of a wisdom beyond human comprehension."[54] *Wyrd*, which is usually taken to mean "whatever happens," is an element of Germanic thought that does not precisely equal the various concepts of fate and fortune discussed in the Latin.[55]

Claims for Alfred's originality are tempered by those who urge readers to analyze his alterations to the Latin source in the context of medieval traditions. The most important study of the context of Alfred's *Consolation* is Otten's, the best book yet written on any of Alfred's translations. Otten discusses the possible impact of Latin commentaries on Alfred's version of the *Consolation* and stresses Alfred's debt to traditional patristic sources.[56] He concludes that Alfred derived many of his ideas from patristic texts and Scripture rather than from the commentaries. The concept that guided Alfred's version, according to Otten, was the "doctrine of merit," a fundamental Christian principle according to which God gives each man his due, punishing the evil and rewarding the good. For Boethius, evil simply did not exist; for Alfred, as Otten writes, "evil is associated with something utterly rotten and depraved, and he shrinks from it almost physically."[57] Otten describes this tension between good and evil, between sin and salvation, as Alfred's "eschatological dualism." Otten is surely correct in maintaining that Alfred understood the role of sin in the world and believed that man's life on earth determined his life in eternity.[58]

No reader of Alfred's version of Boethius can doubt the king's belief in sin and in the forgiveness of sins. Alfred stressed the role of sin and repentance throughout the translation, always to show that man must condition his conduct on earth by his need for eternal salvation. Such a concept is far from Boethius's Neoplatonic prescription that man's life is fated and that at death men are united with the universal good.

Indeed, in Alfred's hand, the *Consolation of Philosophy* became a remarkably religious, even a pious work. Wisdom declares that "vices have need of great repentance, and there is no repentance without sorrow and privation" (chap. 31.1, 70). In the original Lady Philosophy criticizes the pursuit of physical pleasures; to the stricture found in his source Alfred added the warning that pain follows pleasure—that, for example, the pain of childbirth is the punishment of pain that follows a woman's pleasure in sex. Boethius wrote that lust brings sorrow; Alfred more specifically says that vices bring the need for repentance, and repentance brings sorrow and anguish.

In a later, more specific reference to penance Wisdom declares that guilty men should understand "that they might atone for their sins by the punishment that befell them in this world," and should understand this punishment as "cleansing" (chap. 38.4, 120). Wisdom employs a conventional metaphor for confession, saying that the sick one (the sinner) should visit the physician (the confessor) to be made well (chap. 38.7, 123). Among Alfred's other translations, only the *Pastoral Care* refers more often to the need for sins to be forgiven or takes a more stringent attitude toward earthly pleasures.[59] Yet the central theme of Alfred's *Consolation* is not that man should forsake the pleasures of the world—a message Alfred would not have been able to endorse—but instead that he should understand and use them rightly in the search for wisdom.

Alfred's translation of Boethius was shaped by two prevailing influences: his Christian theology, the conventional doctrine of his time, and his practical experience, the distillation of his own observations and discoveries. We find that the translation balances Alfred's Christian beliefs with his practical good sense. Although he denounced covetousness and pride and the abuse of power, Alfred did not denounce power itself; he was not a simple moralist. His most important changes in the *Consolation* reveal a complex attitude that acknowledges but does not seek to resolve the tension between the rewards of this life and the demands of the next.

This tension is what is most attractive about Alfred's recasting of his source. He did not believe that man was fated to a preordained role in the world, but rather that he had the power to make his own world, to do evil or to do good, and that his eternal reward would be the consequence of that choice. In his passionate commitment to learning and to the pursuit of wisdom Alfred valued work not as an end in itself but as a means to a better world. The king's social vision and political philosophy dominate his translation of the *Consolation of Philosophy*. J.M. Wallace-Hadrill is foremost among those who appreciate the influence of political idealism on Alfred's understanding of the text.

What Alfred writes, under the guise of a translation, is a discourse on the pursuit of happiness through obedience to God's will from the standpoint of a ninth-century king, who, through his advisers, has come to see the matter more as Augustine and Gregory the Great saw it. . . . Alfred's *Boethius* is the prime witness to the success of the Church in presenting to the Germanic peoples a theology that took account of their social ideals and made sense of their political organization.[60]

Readers who exaggerate Alfred's similarity to the fallen Boethius forget that Alfred was not a political figure who had lost his power, but a powerful king fully engaged in intellectual, military, and political struggles. Alfred could not regard the trappings of power with the detachment and coldness of an imprisoned Boethius. Alfred was, as Wallace-Hadrill writes, "perfectly clear about the virtue inherent in temporal power, properly exercised under the freedom of choice granted by God as a royal courtesy."[61] Alfred redeemed earthly power not only by making it a reward for wisdom, but by making wisdom and power inseparable. "If you are wise and good," Wisdom tells Mod, "power will follow you even though you do not desire it" (chap. 16, 35). King Alfred already possessed power when he undertook his translation of Boethius's *Consolation*. His long argument about the link between wisdom and true power is both a justification for his own immense power and an appeal to others to search for wisdom, to learn what Alfred was making available to them in their own language. Alfred's translation of the *De Consolatione Philosophiae* could repeat Boethius's denunciation of worldly riches only with many qualifications. Alfred's very occupation of the throne required not that he renounce the world but that he remain in and of the world, live righteously, govern wisely, and use power well.

Chapter Five
The *Soliloquies*: Translation of Augustine

The *Soliloquia* is a dialogue between Augustine and his reason. Alfred's translation of this text, more clearly than any other work attributed to him, reflects the variety of his reading and his preoccupation with the role of learning in shaping man's eternal destiny. Scholars have traditionally assigned the *Soliloquies* to Alfred's last years. The range of sources synthesized in the text suggests that it was written when Alfred's learning had advanced considerably. Some scholars, concluding that questions about immortality in the work express the concerns of an aged and dying king, assume it to have been his last translation.[1] But such speculation, however attractive, encourages a romantic view of Alfred's career and creativity without illuminating the *Soliloquies* or clarifying its chronology in relation to his other works. This text may have been written at the same time as the *Consolation of Philosophy*, which resembles the *Soliloquies*, and the *Soliloquies* may have been written before the translation of the first fifty psalms. Nothing more about the place of the *Soliloquies* in Alfred's canon should be assumed.

Manuscript and Editorial History

The *Soliloquies* exists in only one manuscript, British Library, Cotton Vitellius A.xv, dated mid-twelfth century and hence a late witness to the textual tradition;[2] a prayer which forms part of the first book of the text also exists in a manuscript from the eleventh century, London, British Library, Cotton Tiberius A.iii.[3] The Vitellius manuscript is a composite; the *Soliloquies* is the first item of the first half of the manuscript, which is known as the Southwick Codex. Since the seventeenth century this part of the manuscript has been joined with another collection, the Nowell Codex, which includes *Beowulf* among other Old English prose and poetry.[4]

Unquestionably Alfred's least-studied translation, the *Soliloquies* paradoxically ranks among the most frequently edited of Old English prose texts. Thomas Cockayne's edition in 1864 was followed by those of William Hulme (1893), Henry Hargrove (1902), Wilhelm Endter (1922), and Thomas Carnicelli (1969).[5] This long editorial history records the struggles of scholars with an imperfect manuscript. The *Soliloquies* begins mid-sentence and is, in places, incoherent and obviously incomplete. Possibly the single surviving manuscript was made from an exemplar which itself had lost some leaves before being recopied. Only in this century was the sequence of the latter parts of the text corrected.[6] The gaps in the text are so extensive that the most recent editor's assumption that "the text of the *Soliloquies* is essentially complete as it stands" in the manuscript should be regarded as overly optimistic.[7]

Alfred's Authorship

Claims for Alfred's authorship of the *Soliloquies* depend on three kinds of evidence: a colophon at the end of Book 3, which claims that these "sayings" were gleaned by the king from an unnamed source (the sentence is incomplete);[8] identification of the *Soliloquies* with a handbook supposedly written by Alfred; and linguistic and stylistic analysis.

Neither the colophon nor the link with the handbook establishes Alfred's authorship. The colophon is not necessarily authentic, and may have been added by a later scribe. The assumption that the *Soliloquies* is not a coherent text but a handbook or a collection of "flowers" anthologized by Alfred from different sources has long since been discredited. Asser's *Life* refers to such an anthology as Alfred's *enchiridion*, or handbook. When Asser read something that Alfred especially liked, the king asked that it be copied into his little handbook for future reference; the booklet included psalms, prayers, and sayings that Alfred wished to remember. According to Asser,

Thereafter during our daily discussions, while searching to this end, as we found other equally pleasing passages the quire grew full, and rightly so, just as it is written, "The just man builds on a modest foundation and gradually proceeds to greater things," or like the busy bee, wandering far and wide over the marshes in his quest, eagerly and relentlessly assembles many various flowers of Holy Scripture, with which he crams full the cells of his heart.[9]

In 1877 Wülker suggested that the handbook compiled by Asser and the *Soliloquies* were one and the same.[10] For a time thereafter, until Hargrove's edition appeared in 1902, the work was known as the "Blooms" of King Alfred.[11]

Asser's image of the bee amid the flowers parallels Alfred's use of the word *blostman,* or "blooms," to mark the end of the first book and the beginning and end of the second book. But Asser also reports that Alfred's handbook grew so rapidly that it eventually was nearly as thick as a psalter, the Book of Psalms; the psalms number 150, and bulky psalters possess a heft no manuscript of the *Soliloquies* could have achieved. Nor, as Hargrove observed, is the *Soliloquies* a handbook or "a collection of quotations"; instead, it is "a translation and adaptation of one work," unified by a "dominant theme."[12]

Linguistic and stylistic arguments have now replaced circumstantial claims for Alfred's authorship of the *Soliloquies.* In particular, the text shares important features of vocabulary with other works known to be Alfred's. The evidence of vocabulary, or lexical evidence, enables scholars to group texts which show a shared preference for selecting certain Old English equivalents for Latin terms. Those works accepted as Alfred's frequently exhibit a choice of one Old English word over another, a preference not shared by other works written about the same time.[13] Word choice and syntax in the *Soliloquies* correspond closely to what we find in the *Consolation of Philosophy* and the *Pastoral Care,* works whose ascription to Alfred has rarely if ever been questioned.[14] While this evidence does not firmly fix the chronology of Alfred's canon, it has convinced most scholars that the *Soliloquies* belongs to him.[15]

Augustine: The Latin Source

Neither Augustine's *Soliloquia* nor Alfred's translation of it has earned scholarly esteem. The Latin text has not been reedited since the seventeenth century,[16] although many translations based on this ancient edition are available,[17] and critical commentary is at least adequate.[18] Augustine's text, therefore, is accessible to the student. But the correspondence between the Latin and Alfred's translation cannot be determined because the manuscript tradition of the *Soliloquia* is poorly understood and nothing is known about the form of the Latin text available to Alfred.[19] He may have had a full and accurate copy which he translated freely rather than closely, or he may have faithfully translated a copy that was incomplete and corrupt.

If the medieval tradition of Alfred's Latin source is obscure, the place of the *Soliloquia* itself in Augustine's development is well understood. The text was written after Augustine's conversion but before his baptism, in 387, a period of upheaval in his intellectual development. According to Peter Brown, the *Soliloquia* is "Augustine's first intimate self-portrait, written for a circle of friends."[20] Augustine admitted in his *Retractions* that the *Soliloquia* lacked clarity; but it seems to have satisfied him throughout his life as an early, if inadequate, attempt to combine philosophy with theology and to reconcile Platonic concepts and Christian faith.[21] The *Soliloquia*, written just ten years before the *Confessiones*, has been regarded as its forerunner; the *Soliloquia*, too, is a "sincere and earnest confession of faith," less sophisticated than the *Confessiones* but equally expressive of "a sharp note of unrelieved anxiety and a dependence on God."[22]

At the beginning of Book 1 Augustine states the twin objectives of his search: to know God and to know himself. In the ensuing discussion Reason shows Augustine that knowledge of God is unique and incomparable to other kinds of knowing. Reason compares sight to knowing and reminds Augustine that in order to see objects his eyes must be sound and must be directed in the act of seeing; so too, in order to know God, the mind's eye—that is, Reason—must be healthy, made strong by faith. But Augustine's eyes are not sound. At the end of Book 1 he is still subject to worldly temptations, and still unworthy of the sight of God. Fearing that he will return to the darkness from which he struggles to be free, he pleads for some sign of light. Book 1 concludes with a glimpse of light in the form of Reason's proof that "only immortal things are true." Reason's demonstration of this claim convinces Augustine that he already knows and understands something of immortality, and that he is therefore closer to God than he thought. All that Augustine wishes to understand, Reason promises, will be made clearer to him if he professes himself to be God's servant; God will then draw him nearer to Himself.

Augustine's second book is a detailed discussion of the immortality of the soul and of "our knowing eternally." Augustine himself noted in his *Retractions* that the subject of Book 2 "was not fully dealt with."[23] He continued this theme in another work known as *The Immortality of the Soul* (*De Immortalitate Animae*). This work, published without his consent, was repudiated in the *Retractions* as "so obscure that it is wearisome to read."[24] Alfred's translation refers the reader to another of Augustine's works, *De Videndo Deo*, one of Augustine's letters and one of the sources of Alfred's third book.[25] *De Videndo Deo* appears to have influenced all three books of Alfred's translation of the *Soliloquia*, not just the third.[26] The letter does not directly address the question of immortality, which Alfred made the focus of Book 3; rather, many of its chapters discuss the problem of knowing God through the senses, an issue explored throughout the *Soliloquia*.[27]

Alfred's Translation: An Overview

Alfred's translation comprises three books preceded by a lengthy preface which has no counterpart in the original. This preface, and many additions to the text which follow, suggest that Alfred sought to develop a work different in scope and character from Augustine's, and focused on issues not raised in the Latin. We do not know if Alfred and his helpers worked from a complete Latin text, or if they had access to a commentary on Augustine's work and derived some observations on the text from that source. Therefore, our observations about the "originality" of Alfred's text cannot be verified.

But we can at least be sure that the king did not follow Augustine's pattern closely or translate Augustine's work literally; Alfred's aim was less to duplicate Augustine's achievement than to adapt it to his own concerns. The reader has little difficulty in following the Latin discussion, apart from the abstraction of the subject matter, but the Old English text contains detours and distractions, most of them created by analogies that Alfred and his helpers introduced. As the translators enriched the Latin, they extended the text in uncertain directions and elevated minor issues to primary status, thereby thoroughly altering Augustine's meaning.

The preface. Alfred's preface is an allegory about writing and learning. The king describes himself as a woodsman traveling to the forest to secure posts, lumber, and other building materials for a house. On every tree he has seen "something that I needed at home," and he exhorts everyone who is able to follow him likewise to "load his [wagons] with fair twigs" so that he too can build a house, a "fair dwelling" to inhabit both in winter and in summer "as I have not yet done" (47). Two images dominate this passage: the timber-gatherer and cottage-builder. Together they describe a process of assimilation and reformulation that is itself an apt metaphor for Alfred's translation. The timber in the forest comprises the ideas of the Latin fathers, some of them—Augustine, Gregory, and Jerome—named in the pref-

ace, whose works Alfred combed for important ideas; the house built
of the timber represents Alfred's reconstruction of those thoughts into
his own concepts. In the forest he acquires knowledge; in the cottage
he finds two uses for it: to enjoy life in this world, and to pursue
salvation and happiness in the next. The "temporary cottage" serves
as a way station for those traveling to the everlasting kingdom (47).
God eases the pilgrimage of life in this world by providing the cottage as both a place of rest on the journey and a place of prayer and
learning. Its initial purpose is to offer man a respite from worldly
toil; its ultimate purpose is to help him save his soul.

Man's rest in the cottage is no idle relaxation but a retreat to meditation. Once in the cottage, man concerns himself with the land and
sea around it. Alfred stresses that the occupant should take pleasure
in his dwelling place and in his work and recreation. These satisfac-
tions should encourage him to think of more permanent residency.
While a man may rest in the cottage, built "on his lord's lease and
by his help," he also uses his time there to gain ownership of the land
(known in Alfred's time as "fee simple") and to enjoy the surrounding
region, hunting and fishing as he pleases.

Alfred says that "every man, when he has, with his lord's help,
built a hamlet on land leased by his lord, likes to stay there some
time," and enjoy himself, and "employ himself on that leased land,
both on sea and land, until the time when he shall deserve bookland"
(48). Bookland, a technical term in the Anglo-Saxon legal vocabulary,
refers to a form of land tenure in which noblemen left land to the
Church for the good of their souls.[28] To "deserve bookland" means to
inherit that land rightfully, to possess it and its accompanying privi-
leges. "Leased land" is a temporary arrangement necessary for life in
this world; "bookland" is a permanent reward which represents life in
the world to come.

Book 1.   At the end of the preface Alfred says that Augustine,
bishop of Carthage, "made two books about his own mind" concerning "the meditation and doubts of his mind." In these books "Reason
answered his mind when that mind doubted something, or wished to
know something that it could not previously comprehend clearly"
(48). Alfred now assumes the role of Augustine, and the dialogue begins. (For the sake of clarity, we will distinguish Alfred's Augustine
from the speaker Augustine in the Latin original.)

Book 1 may be divided into three parts. In the first, Alfred's Augustine, prodded by Reason, states that his wish is to understand

God and his own soul. In the second part, Reason explains what qualities are necessary before the eye can see or the mind can understand God; this section develops extensive analogies between sight and understanding. The third part renews the quest begun in the first but reveals that the present moral state of Alfred's Augustine does not permit him to understand God. This frustrating revelation is tempered when Reason saves Alfred's Augustine from despair by showing him that he already understands something of God because he understands something of immortality, itself the subject of Book 2.

The theme of Alfred's translation emerges at the beginning of Book 1, where the speaker asks "whether his mind and his soul were mortal and transitory" (49). Alfred introduces this question about immortality, which is not found in the original; in the Latin, the speaker speculates about good and evil and about how man is to do one and avoid the other. Augustine inquired into the nature of good and evil, Alfred into the meaning of immortality. As he questions Reason, Alfred's Augustine constantly seeks reassurance that man, knowing God but imperfectly in this life, and constantly distracted from the pursuit of wisdom, can nonetheless hope to be saved.

Reason asks Augustine to which faculty he would commit all that he learns so that he could both retain it and continue to "go on with other things." In the Latin, Augustine replies that he must commit all "to the memory."[29] Alfred's Augustine, like his namesake, learns that his memory cannot "both always keep watch and ward over that which you have acquired, and also get more" wisdom (49). He must write what he has learned so that he can retain what has been learned while he acquires new wisdom. But, before Alfred's Augustine can write, Reason offers advice: "[you need] a few wise and skillful men with you who would not hinder you at all but help you with your task" (49). Alfred's Augustine laments that he has no such assistance—a reminder of the comment attributed to Alfred in Asser's *Life*, that the king had no teachers when he was young and at leisure, and no leisure when he was older and had teachers.[30]

Seeking to console him, Reason tells Augustine to pray. Much expanded from the Latin source, Alfred's prayer asks for faith and for good teaching so that Augustine can know "what is best and most righteous for me in this life" (56). In the Latin, Augustine's prayer recalls the Platonic concept according to which all things at death return to their place of origin. For Augustine, this Platonic harmony in creation illustrates God's governance of the world. The seasons revolve, and "over longer periods there is the perfection of the course of the sun, and in their vast circles the stars return to the place of their rising."[31]

Alfred's Augustine does not repeat this description but observes that some things "change in another way, so that the same ones do not come again to where they were before, or indeed become what they were." They are instead replaced by others—as apples are replaced on the tree, as men's bodies grow old and age—and arise to new life in which they do not change (53). By his addition, Alfred seeks to prove that Augustine's generalization is not true to experience; because they wither and die, neither the bodies nor the apples become what they once were. The alteration of the Latin source cannot be explained as an attempt to exemplify Augustine's point or to make it concrete. While he does not deny the truth of Augustine's statement, Alfred sharply qualifies it, simultaneously pointing beyond it to a larger truth not discussed in the Latin—the resurrection of the soul to eternal life.

Alfred's qualification of Augustine's observation about the harmony of creation does not seem to intensify piety, even though it appears midway in a prayer. Instead, the addition acknowledges an easily observed phenomenon of natural decay that happens to contradict the spirit of the Latin source. Alfred seems not to have attached great value to either the form or the character of the original at this point; he did not hesitate to sacrifice the conventions of prayer to his own perceptions of reality. This change is Alfred's first use in this text of empirical observation to check abstract theory; similar changes occur throughout. Although his alterations of the prayer set the direction for his revision of Augustine's work, most of Alfred's petition follows the Latin source closely.

Asked what he "most needs and requires to know," Alfred's Augustine replies, "to understand God and know mine own soul" (56). Before the search can begin, he must have a standard for measuring what he knows; without that benchmark, he will not know when he has learned what he wishes to learn. Reason introduces extended analogies that pose the knowledge of God in terms of understanding acquired through the senses—knowledge of another person (a servant), future events, geometry, and astronomical bodies. Most of these analogies appear in some form in the Latin, but the central analogy in the original incorporates an elaborate discussion of geometry. Alfred did not duplicate the geometrical analogy, possibly because he thought it was too technical—and even too tedious—for his audience.[32]

Alfred replaces the geometric analogy with a simpler and more direct one. Instead of a long discussion of bisecting lines on spheres, we find a discussion about ships and virtue. Just as one arrives on land by means of a ship, but must then abandon the ship and proceed to traverse the land without it, one learns at first by looking with the eyes, and thereafter by contemplating with the mind (61). Alfred's Augustine knows that one more easily pulls a ship across land than understands science with the eyes only, without using reason. Therefore, he must look "straight with the eyes of the mind to God"; he must use reason in his attempt to see God. Just as an anchor cable holds a ship fast to land, sight fastens the mind to God (61). When Alfred's Augustine asks for a definition of the mind's eyes, Reason replies that they are Reason "in addition to other virtues" which include wisdom, humility, honor, temperance, righteousness, mildheartedness, prudence, constancy, good will, and chastity (62). Wishing to submit to Reason's teaching, Augustine remains troubled; he cannot understand how he can acquire these anchors. Reason replies that to renounce vices is to acquire virtues, for vices anchor man to earth, and when one forsakes them, he becomes anchored to God (62).

Stressing the difficulty of shedding old habits, Alfred's Augustine appears torn between his allegiance to the reality around him, which he knows and believes in, and his desire to be saved, a desire staked on the unknown and unknowable. The tension between what is known by the senses and what can be accepted only by faith is a dominant theme of Alfred's text. In order to illustrate this tension Reason resorts to a parable. Reason asks Alfred's Augustine if, possessing certain gifts from his lord, he would choose that wealth over a new expression of his lord's will if it arrived in a sealed letter. Augustine replies that he would choose the giver—that is, would follow the command in the letter, his lord's intent—rather than keep the gifts (62). When one's lord announces his intention anew, one should not cling to rewards previously bestowed merely because they are known and readily available. Then, by analogy, Reason compares the speaker's earthly wealth, the temporal gift of his earthly lord, to the gifts of his heavenly lord, described as the anchors of virtue, which, Reason says, are eternal. If Alfred's Augustine prizes the friendship of this lord, he should value more highly still the friendship of the heavenly lord, who rules over all and whose gifts last forever. The known, therefore, should encourage Augustine to seek the unknown of surpassing worth.

In the second part of Book 1 Reason expounds on its own powers through extensive visual analogies which are linked to the discussion of virtues just concluded. Alfred's Augustine learns that "the mind is the eye of the soul" and that Reason is "to every human mind what looking is to the eyes" (65). These "eyes" are the virtues of faith, hope, and charity; lacking them no soul has sound sight. If Augustine can see clearly, he can know, for "seeing is knowing" (66).[33] The vision of God is knowledge which links the one who understands to that which is understood, Reason explains, just as love links the lover and the loved one, and just as the cable links the anchor to the ship.

With perfect knowledge, man needs only love, for love alone increases "when the understanding is fixed on God"; unlike faith and hope, love has no end (67). But man's soul, encumbered by the body, cannot see God without much labor through hope and faith to attain love. Alfred attempted to clarify this continuation of his discussion of virtue with another nautical analogy, comparing the virtues that join man to God with the anchor that steadies the ship amid stormy waves. The mind, anchored by virtue, is comforted in distress with the knowledge that misfortunes are not eternal (68). If man believes in God and asks God for help, God will give him hope, and God will work His will through man, making man His tool and His "coworker" in performing God's will in the world.[34]

Alfred's Augustine receives this instruction gladly, but returns to his first questions about acquiring knowledge of God and himself: he knows what he ought to do, but not whether he can accomplish it. Reason introduces yet another analogy, comparing the truth which man struggles to comprehend to the sun. Reason says that Augustine can observe three things about the sun: that it exists, that it shines, and that it illuminates other things (69). Alfred's Reason elaborates, noting that various objects reflect the sun differently, some brightly, some not at all. While no one can see the sun perfectly, everyone rejoices in being able to see it somewhat; likewise, man can see God only imperfectly (70).

Reason has promised that Augustine shall see God with the eyes of his mind as clearly as he sees the sun with bodily eyes. Three problems trouble Augustine and hinder his pursuit of wisdom: parting from friends, enduring sickness, and suffering death (71). Reason interprets these distractions as indications of what Augustine most values—friends, his own health, and his own life—and says that they should come after God and Reason in importance (71). Because Augustine does not have all his friends and because his health is poor, he is downcast. It is, Reason says, folly to try to see the sun with eyes so sick—that is, to try to comprehend God when one is beset by worldly cares (72).

Having diagnosed Augustine's disability, Reason begins the third section of Book 1 with an inquiry into Augustine's moral life. Attempting to find what distracts Alfred's Augustine, Reason asks about his love of wealth, honor, and women, finding that Augustine has rejected them all. But Alfred's Augustine does have material needs, and expresses special concern for the needs of those whose care is his duty—those, we may assume, who rely on the king for their well-being (73). Augustine wishes to retain his friends because he loves them (74), prompting Reason to explore these attachments to friends and friendship as possible temptations to greed and covetousness.

As Reason probes Augustine's motives for loving his friends, a major theme of Alfred's *Soliloquies* emerges. In the Latin, Reason asks Augustine why, if he wishes to be free of all that impedes the search for wisdom, he wishes to have his friends with him. Augustine says that his friends help him and teach him. If having friends should keep him from pursuing wisdom, Augustine would temporize: "We shall do the best we can." When Reason asks a second time whether Augustine will continue with his friends if they hinder him, he admits that he would leave his friends should they become a burden in his search for wisdom. Reason concludes that he desires "their life and presence not for their own sake, but in order to find out wisdom."[35]

In his replies to Reason Alfred's Augustine affirms friendship much more vigorously than does the original Augustine. Alfred's Augustine declares that he would keep his friends even if they should create difficulties, since "they are useful to me for some things," and he likewise to them. If his friends complicate the search for wisdom, he wants to have them anyway. He loves those friends who help him find wisdom, and even those who do not do so help him in other ways; he replies, "Nevertheless I will have them" (74). The Old English text is defective at this point; apparently missing is Augustine's reply to Reason's second question, which in the Latin prompted Augustine's denial of his friends. Possibly, Alfred followed suit and dismissed his friends as a hindrance to wisdom. But Alfred translated Augustine's equivocal reply to the first question—"we shall do our best"—as a strong affirmation of friendship: "I will have them." This affirmation reasserts a temporal value against a spiritual concept, again exemplifying Alfred's high estimation of a social good—in this case, loyalty to friends—and his refusal to subordinate that earthly good to an abstract value.

Reason tests Augustine's commitment to the search for wisdom and repeatedly shows Augustine that earthly attachments, including friendship, impede that search. Reason argues that if Augustine wishes to have wisdom he cannot allow anything to stand between himself and it, just as no cloth can stand between the hand and the body it wishes to caress (75). But Alfred's Augustine replies that he loves wisdom above all else, as Reason has told him he must (76). Alfred's Augustine cannot separate the search for wisdom from his love of friendship, for he loves all men who help him find wisdom, and wishes that all men might discover wisdom and find unity in the love of wisdom. Alfred creates a defense of friendship far more vigorous and entrenched than that found in his source.

Reason concludes the argument of Book 1 with a series of analogies that show that all men who wish to approach wisdom can do so. All men may approach their lord's home, but they come from varying distances, some with ease, some with difficulty (77). Likewise, the sharpness of a man's vision—his ability to grasp wisdom—depends on the soundness of his eyes.[36] Reason also says that one finds wisdom gradually, step by step, just as one would use a ladder to climb a cliff (78). The objective of Book 1 has been to show the many ways in which Augustine's eyes are sick. Thus, Reason reminds Alfred's Augustine that men with unsound eyes need teachers, for the physician knows better than the sick man how he can be healed (79). But he should not despair because he cannot see wisdom itself, for his eyes are not as whole as he had supposed. If he will restrain his weeping, he will be shown a shorter way to wisdom.

Because Alfred's Augustine still wishes to know what he asked to know before—about God and his own soul (81)—Reason asks him if he thinks that truth and the true are one and the same. Augustine replies that they are not the same; virtue must be distinguished from the virtuous one, wisdom separated from the one who is wise, and chastity separated from the one who is chaste. Alfred's Augustine realizes that virtuous men pass away but that virtues do not. His earthly gifts are necessary and useful, but they should not impede his search for wisdom, which is a gift that will never desert him. When Augustine confesses faith in the lasting quality of God's gifts, Reason urges him to believe firmly in God and to commit himself wholly to God as His servant. Any adversity that God should permit Augustine to suffer will be for his good. Thus the "anthology" of the first book ends with a strong appeal to faith and with Reason's request that Augustine express any remaining doubts about what he has learned in the first book.

Book 2. Alfred's second book, less than one-third the length of the first, is much simpler in design and content. Alfred acknowledges Augustine's concern with the immortality of the soul, the announced topic of Book 2 in the original, in which Augustine repeats that he wishes to know God and himself. But Alfred's translation soon departs widely from its source. As Carnicelli, Whitelock, and others have noted, however, Alfred returned to the end of Augustine's second book to end his own.[37]

Reason asks Augustine if he knows that he exists and lives; Augustine answers affirmatively and adds that he wishes to know if he is also immortal. At this point Alfred introduces his own concern into Book 2, his Augustine explaining that he most wishes to know

Whether I shall live forever, and whether, after the parting of the body and the soul, I shall ever know more than I now know of all that I have long wished to know; for I cannot find anything better in man than that he know, and nothing worse than that he be ignorant. (84)

Concluding that Augustine wishes to live so that he may know, Reason, in the translation, states that Augustine loves "wisdom above all other things" (85). That wisdom is the highest good—the prevailing theme of Book 1—emerges in Book 2 in a new context. Alfred's Augustine knows that he exists and that he knows at least something, although not all that he wishes to know. Reason asks if he also wishes to know if his existence, his life, and his desire to know will continue beyond the grave (85).

Although Reason amply demonstrates that the soul is immortal, Augustine continues to question that assertion, finally asking that he be able to know, rather than merely believe, this truth. Reason appeals to God and the Apostles as sources of wisdom which Augustine cannot reject, and then asks Augustine how he would receive some news from his lord that he, Augustine, did not know. This example recalls the sealed letter in Book 1, another analogy for the acceptance on faith of a truth that cannot be independently verified. Alfred's Augustine replies that "there is no story so incredible that if he told it, I would not believe him" (88). Indeed, he would believe the story if he heard it from his companions instead of his lord himself. Reason applauds Augustine's faith in his friends and constructs an analogy based on this trust, concluding that if Augustine will accept his friends' testimony for the will of an earthly lord, he should also accept the testimony of numerous holy men concerning the will of the heavenly king (88).

Having established in Augustine's mind the immortality of the soul, Reason describes death and resurrection as a process in which the soul, adorned and beautified, loses its beauty and then regains it. The renewability of the soul and the cycle of recreation and rebirth, Boethian themes introduced into the prayer in Book 1, reemerge in Book 2, again subjects of a passage Alfred apparently added to the original. At the end of Book 2 Augustine willingly accepts Reason's proofs, agreeing that the soul and the intellect are both eternal. But he repeats his question concerning the intellect, whether it shall, "after the parting of the body and the soul, wax or wane, or shall remain in one place, or do as it did previously in this world—wax for a time, and then wane" (91). Reason refers the reader to *De Videndo Deo*, the primary source of Book 3 and the second of Augustine's works that Alfred consulted in translating the *Soliloquies*.

Book 3.   Serious defects in the manuscript compromise the clarity of Book 3 of Alfred's translation.[38] Alfred's Augustine repeats his question about the immortality of knowing. In a passage reminiscent of many Old English texts about the Last Judgment, Reason describes the torment of the wicked, which shall increase the reward of the good. Reason declares that those who toiled on earth to learn shall know more in the next life, and shall have "likewise more honor and more glory" (94). Alfred's Augustine establishes a direct correlation between the pursuit of wisdom in this life and one's reward in the life to come. This link forms a powerful justification for studying wisdom and, of course, from the point of view of Alfred's audience, for heeding the king's word. Alfred's Augustine accepts Reason's teaching and states his own belief that wisdom is not lost after death, but rather increased. Saying that his questions are now answered, Augustine states that he has learned by example and by "sacred books," testimony too reliable to reject (94).

After a break in the text, Reason reminds Alfred's Augustine that the soul is weighed down by the body and that the body keeps the soul from knowing all that it would know, including God.[39] The sight metaphor, which appeared in Book 1, appears here in a negative context: just as clouds sometimes block the sun, man's body impairs his "mind's eye"—his Reason, as defined in Book 1. But after Doomsday, when the soul escapes from the prison of the body, man shall know all that he wishes to know, more than even the wisest of the ancients knew. He shall see God openly and the sight of Him shall be a reward to the good and a punishment to the evil (93).

The dialogue between Reason and Alfred's Augustine ends abruptly. Book 3 concludes with a third-person narrative in which Alfred explores the implications of increased knowledge after death. The sudden shift from dialogue to discourse testifies to the incompleteness of the *Soliloquies*. Having progressed well beyond the limits of Augustine's original text, Alfred abandoned the dialogue device in favor of a straightforward discussion of his own chief concerns.

Drawing on Gregory the Great's *Dialogi* and *Regula Pastoralis* rather than on Augustine's works, Alfred retells the parable of Lazarus and Dives. He uses the narrative to ask if it is possible that the good have after death no memory of their friends.[40] Dives remembered his friends after his death and sought consolation from them. When he realized that he could not have Lazarus to console him, he asked that Lazarus should go to his brothers on Dives' behalf. But Lazarus was forbidden to do so because the brothers, the Lord assured him, would not believe his story. Alfred uses the parable to establish two points: first, that the dead see this life and remember their kinsmen and friends; second, that the good help the good after death, but have no mercy on the evil, and that the evil cannot help themselves or others after death because they do no good while they are alive.

In his conclusion Alfred asserts that the righteous, from their position in eternity, will reflect on the good and evil that they did in this life and will be glad that they did not stray from their Lord's will. Then, once again constructing an analogy based on royal power, Alfred discusses the soul's return to God in the afterlife. A king may drive away one of his favorites, or a favored retainer may have been separated from the king against both their wills. When the exile returns to the king, the reunion is joyous for both. In this analogy the exile returned is the soul returned to heaven, increasing the pleasure taken in its newfound happiness by remembering its former misery.

In another abrupt shift—this one not created by a gap in the manuscript[41]—Alfred affirms his belief in many things that he has not seen. He thereby raises the question of whom to believe or to trust. Someone must be trusted, and that person's word accepted on faith. Just as Alfred accepts the foundation of Rome on faith, so too must he use faith to accept other truths. His response to the speculative issues raised in the third book is that only faith can reconcile man to truths that cannot be confirmed. His concluding observation injects a private and personal spirit into Book 3 and casts new light on his belief in the immortality of the soul, the major question of Book 2. Book 3 reaffirms the earlier argument and restates it more simply. Despite all that has been said earlier about the use of wisdom to confirm belief, Alfred knows of his own begetting not because he saw it but because of hearsay, because it was told to him. All knowledge of the issues raised in the *Soliloquies*—immortality, the understanding of God and of man's soul, and the eternal quality of knowing—must be accepted on faith alone.

The Relation of the *Soliloquies* to the *Consolation of Philosophy*

Discussion of the critical tradition of King Alfred's *Soliloquies* should be prefaced by a review of efforts to clarify the relation of this work to the *Consolation of Philosophy*. Scholars of Alfred's *Soliloquies* face few more difficult challenges. The two texts are traditionally said to be very close; both are dialogues and, although their themes are quite different, both explore the problem of man's search for happiness in this world and for his salvation in the next. The *Soliloquies* dates from Augustine's early, predominantly philosophical period and concerns itself with some of the same philosophical issues that appear in the *Consolation*. But neither Augustine's nor Boethius's text is wholly theological or philosophical.

We should remember that Alfred's version of the *Consolation* was "Christianized" by commentaries, or by additions by Alfred himself from Christian sources, and for this reason is less philosophical and more theological than the Latin original. At the same time, the king's translation of the *Soliloquies*, while no less theological than its Latin source, frequently interjects observations—for example, about friendship—that subordinate theology to a more practical philosophical perspective. E. T. Silk long ago suggested that the *De Consolatione Philosophiae* was written partially under the influence of Augustine's work, not only of the *Confessiones* but also, perhaps, of the *Soliloquia*.[42] Although Boethius was a Christian (one of his conflicts with Theodoric was that the emperor persisted in the Arian heresy, while Boethius represented the conservative Catholic thought of the Roman aristocracy), his "real religion," as the nineteenth-century historian Edward Zeller said, was philosophy.[43] Admittedly, the influence of the *Soliloquia* on Boethius is second to that of the *Confessiones*, which, according to a recent study, "should be numbered among the most important influences" on the *De Consolatione*.[44] But the *Soliloquia* and the *Confessiones* are themselves closely related by scholars of Augustine.[45] Therefore, scholars seeking to determine the chronology of Alfred's translations of the *Soliloquia* and the *De Consolatione Philosophiae* find their task complicated by a close but unclarified connection between Alfred's Latin sources.

The traditional assumption is that Alfred first wrote the *Consolation* and that he borrowed parts of the *Soliloquies* from it. But we do not know the Latin form of either text as Alfred might have received it; therefore, in neither case can we identify with certainty all the material that he and his helpers added to their sources. Some passages common to the texts derive from the Latin original of one or the other; other common passages are additions by Alfred and his helpers. Before we can compare the texts, we have to be certain which text served as a source for the other. If a passage in the *Soliloquies* can be shown to derive from material that we know Alfred added to the *Consolation*, then we have established two reasonably certain points: first, that Alfred wrote both texts and, second, that he produced his translation of the *Consolation* first and used it, rather than the *De Consolatione*, as a source for the *Soliloquies*. However, if a passage from the *Soliloquies* is found in the *De Consolatione* as well as in Alfred's translation of Boethius, then the translator of the *Soliloquies* may have known Boethius in the Latin only. In that case, we have established nothing certain about either common authorship or the sequence of Alfred's translations.

Because material that Alfred added to the *Consolation* is, in several instances, also added to the *Soliloquies*, scholars have concluded that the *Soliloquies* borrows from the translation of the *Consolation*.[46] The view that the *Soliloquies* was influenced by Alfred's translation of Boe-

thius was first offered by Frank G. Hubbard.[47] Carnicelli lists some
of the topics common to the texts in his review of the evidence, and,
with few qualifications, supports Hubbard's conclusion that the translation of Boethius was the "earlier work."[48] The material common to
the texts includes God's ordering of the world in cyclical patterns;
nautical analogies; analogies involving the sun and eyesight; comparisons between men's and angels' souls; and friendship.[49] Because many
of these passages are regarded as original to the *Soliloquies*, and because they correspond to passages translated from the *Consolation*,
scholars have generally agreed that Alfred translated the Boethius
first.

Despite its obvious merit, this view creates certain problems. As
both Hubbard and Carnicelli recognized, the correspondences do not
unanimously favor an earlier date for the Boethian text. To establish
borrowing—that is, the dependence of the *Soliloquies* on the *Consolation*—one must demonstrate verbal parallels so close that neither coincidence nor other sources can account for the resemblance. Not all
the passages said to link these translations pass this strict verbal test.
Those passages that correspond most closely are derived from the
Latin source of each translation.[50]

Moreover, at least one passage in the Boethius may be derived from
the *Soliloquies*. This passage states that a man with unhealthy eyes
must look on objects of increasing brightness—gold, silver, fire—before he can see the sun.[51] The passage is an addition to the *Consolation*,
but it is found in the Latin original of the *Soliloquies*. This evidence
cannot be lightly dismissed, even though Carnicelli regards it as a
parallel "more of thought than of phrasing."[52] Indeed, the same opinion might justly be applied to several of the correspondences that Carnicelli and others see as proving the dependence of the *Soliloquies* on
the *Consolation*.

The traditional explanations do not adequately demonstrate the pri-
ority of the *Consolation*. Indeed, it could be argued that the *Soliloquies*
influenced the translation of the *Consolation*. Alfred changed the
names of the speakers in the latter dialogue in a way that suggests
that he knew of Augustine's text when he began to translate the *De
Consolatione*. In both Augustine's text and Alfred's translation of it
Augustine speaks to Reason. In the *De Consolatione* the teacher of Boethius is known as Lady Philosophy. But, in Alfred's translation, she
is known either as Reason or as Wisdom, and her partner is known
first as Boethius, then as "Mod" or "Mind," and finally as "I." The

change of names in the *Consolation* may at least in part be explained by Alfred's familiarity with Augustine's text when he began to work with Boethius. Given the length of the *De Consolatione* and the complexity of the *Soliloquia*, Alfred may well have worked on the translations simultaneously over a period of months or even years. Our attempts to determine the sequence of these two translations should not omit the possibility that they were undertaken simultaneously.[53] Alfred may have found the texts together in a collection of dialogues and translated the *Soliloquies* and the *Consolation* as a complementary pair.

Critical Trends

The most recent critical discussions of the *Soliloquies* focus on matters of internal coherence and integrity, especially the unity of the text and its accuracy as an interpretation of Augustine's argument. Hargrove sketched a topos still useful in analyzing the *Soliloquies*: he saw Alfred as the translator of Book 1, the adapter of Book 2, and the author of Book 3.[54] Virtually all subsequent studies acknowledge the same gradation in Alfred's contribution to the text.

But the unity of the *Soliloquies* remains problematical. Even though the work is no longer identified with the "handbook" mentioned by Asser, Wrenn describes the text as a "collection of freely rendered passages . . . together with reflections and meditations on them" called blossoms.[55] Greenfield calls the work a "chrestomathy, or a gathering of blooms or flowers."[56] These characterizations respond not only to discontinuities in the text but also to the variety of sources that Alfred attempted to synthesize into a coherent argument. The work collects ideas drawn from Augustine, Gregory, Jerome, and other fathers of the church cited in the preface to the translation (47), and even the most sympathetic reader must admit that Alfred failed both to render Augustine's text accurately and to achieve a consistent focus of his own. The *Soliloquies* draws from the widest range of sources of any of Alfred's translations. Chief among these is his own translation of Boethius; also included are Gregory the Great's *Dialogi*, *Regula Pastoralis*, *Moralia*, and *Homilia in Evangelia*, Augustine's *De Videndo Deo*, possibly *De Civitate Dei*, and a text once thought to have been written by Jerome, *Expositio Quattuor Evangeliorum*.[57] But Alfred's synthetic method did not prevent him from fashioning a reasonably coherent statement about the immortality of the soul and the role of learning in helping man comprehend God both in this life and the next. Alfred's statement is simply different from Augustine's, and less elegantly conceived.

Recent discussions have reacted to arguments against the unity of the *Soliloquies* by forcefully asserting its coherence. Gatch has studied the rationale behind Alfred's translation and concluded that it "has greater unity and completeness than its chief original source."[58] Ruth Waterhouse has analyzed tone in the work and approached it for the first time as a consistent, literary production. But she admits that Alfred "sometimes loses the thread of the intellectual argument in his desire to develop the metaphors [of the Latin] into new aspects of the basic idea," and that his additions sometimes spoil "the overall coherence of the whole group [of metaphors]."[59]

A reasonably strong defense of the coherence of the *Soliloquies* can be derived from Alfred's preface, the most important and original section of the work, and a richer source of information about the translator's literary methods and his attitude toward learning than any of his writings except the preface to the *Pastoral Care*. Unlike the earlier preface, the preface to the *Soliloquies* has rarely been scrutinized as a statement about Alfred's concept of literature and education. Even though our version of it is incomplete, it offers a satisfying unifying scheme for the entire text.[60] Alfred's *Soliloquies* brings together many ideas: his preoccupations with learning and the role of learning in shaping man's eternal destiny, and his concern with friendship, immortality, and good government. These are, in short, all the themes for which his other writings are known; their synthesis in the *Soliloquies* begins with the preface.

There Alfred compares himself to a woodsman who gathers building materials in the forest. He also pictures himself as a tenant who builds a cottage on his lord's land as a place for rest and recreation. As Gatch claims, we find here Alfred's plan for the work. Gatch argues that the "writing of a vernacular version of the *Soliloquies* is but one instance of the gathering of material from the forest of Christian knowledge for the building of one's heavenly habitation." Gatch further observes that "Alfred attempted to use the Augustinian wood to build a unified structure that would help man and his soul in the quest for salvation."[61] The timbers form a "unified structure," the *Soliloquies*, to be used in saving one's soul: ideas found in the text build a pattern for life, and man uses the ideas by figuratively living within their confines, following ideals, and adhering to Christian beliefs.

However, if Alfred's thoughts never stray far from the eternal reality of salvation, neither does he disregard or devalue the world's pleasures and necessities. The Christian wisdom of Alfred's writing derives its character chiefly from this reluctance to ignore, much less condemn outright, the pleasures of life in the world. Alfred's attempt to reconcile the physical and the spiritual may be seen as a governing concept behind the *Soliloquies*.

Alfred weaves the truth of his own experience into the Augustinian argument. For him the search for wisdom demands that one appreciate, understand, and embrace what is around him. And sometimes the strands of his own experience and commonsense conclusions do not fit into the Augustinian pattern. But the discord they create can be tolerated, for the *Soliloquies* is synthetic in nature and purpose. Translating this text allowed Alfred to test against his own experience Augustine's abstract, ideal statement about the role of wisdom in the world. At points Alfred seems to have concluded that the theory of Augustine did not coincide with the practice of government. Many of Alfred's changes reflect the reality of experience and simple good sense about events in the natural world; in those changes we see the king's extreme reluctance, finally his refusal, to set empiricism aside in favor of abstract reasoning. He was unwilling to reject experience and the earthly attachments that, for Augustine, impeded the search for wisdom.

Perhaps the clearest demonstration of Alfred's empiricism and his practical good sense is his assertion of friendship against the strictures of Augustine. As we see in the preface, friends were not merely useful in Alfred's search for wisdom: they were essential, for without companions to aid him in his work, Alfred could not have undertaken this translation, much less an entire program of educational renewal. While Augustine rejects the rewards of friendship when they begin to compromise the search for wisdom, Alfred does not. He discusses friendship in every section of the *Soliloquies*, especially in the preface and in Books 1 and 3, repeatedly reaffirming its value. He allows for the possibility of forsaking one's friends only in Book 3, and there he states that friendship forges a meaningful link between good men even after death (96).

Like other important changes—the discussion of the revolution of the seasons, or the numerous nautical and political analogies—Alfred's discussion of friendship may be original with him or may reflect a lost source which supplemented his text of Augustine. In either case, Alfred's text shares little with Augustine's, in form or in spirit. Perhaps the most important of the factors that explain the king's divergence from his source is the private and personal subject matter of the *Soliloquies*, a work that comes closer to spiritual autobiography than any other he translated.

Alfred's changes in the *Soliloquia* cannot readily be characterized or categorized, but many of them express an underlying insistence that one cannot reject the world, or retreat to a cottage of other men's ideas, without neglecting moral obligations to the community, to followers, and to oneself. Much as he appears to have longed for solitude, for good teachers, and for a sabbatical from the pressures of government, Alfred judged that the business of life wisely led must sometimes take precedence over the pursuit of philosophical ideas.

Chapter Six
The *Paris Psalter*:
Translation of the Psalms

Although each of King Alfred's works has brought us into contact
with literature from cultures older and richer than his own, none recapitulates a literary history more comprehensively than his translation of the first fifty psalms. These Old Testament poems originated
in Hebrew and were, centuries later, translated into Greek and Latin;
they were then enveloped in Christian meaning through the exegetical
commentaries of the early church fathers.

Biblical scholars have puzzled over the psalms for centuries, but
Anglo-Saxonists have only begun to investigate Alfred's treatment of
them, for only recently has his authorship of the first fifty psalms in
the *Paris Psalter* been established. As a result, they have been studied
less than most of his other works; their editorial history and critical
tradition are sparse, and their relation to Alfred's other writing has
barely been investigated. His contribution to the *Paris Psalter* is both
the most underrated of his translations and the ripest for critical inquiry, for it incorporates a complex tradition of psalter study in the
early Middle Ages and yet treats the sacred ancient text distinctively.

Manuscript and Editorial History

The prose psalms comprise the first third of the *Paris Psalter*, a
manuscript of the mid-eleventh century, which contains all 150
psalms in Latin and Old English.[1] The manuscript has curious dimen-
sions: over 21 inches high but only 7 inches wide; the text occupies
two columns on each page, the Latin text on the left, the Old English
on the right.[2] Each of the fifty prose psalms, except the first, is preceded by a short introduction which explains how the psalm is to be
interpreted. The remaining psalms are translated into verse, without
introductions.

The prose and verse translations have different authors and were written at different times; the meter of the verse is irregular and appears to be dated late (that is, tenth century or after), while the prose is unquestionably from Alfred's period.[3] The Latin text was not the source of either the verse or the prose translation, since the Latin text differs from both and seems to be later than either.[4] The compiler of this manuscript apparently began with a Latin text of the psalms and Alfred's translation of the first fifty of them, and then, to complete the bilingual psalter, appended the remaining one hundred psalms from a verse translation. Several versified psalters survive in fragmentary form, but we do not know which verse translation Alfred used.[5]

Of Alfred's translations, only the *Soliloquies* is so poorly attested in manuscripts as the *Paris Psalter*. Both exist in unique copies, and as a result we are unable to trace the development of the text through its manuscript history. The introductions to the prose psalms also appear in a Winchester manuscript of the mid-eleventh century,[6] but this copy was not made from the *Paris Psalter*; instead, both manuscripts have a common ancestor.[7] The Paris manuscript is imperfect. Two folios are missing between the end of Psalm 50.8 (the last in prose) and Psalm 51.7 (the first in verse); other gaps leave us with incomplete introductions to several psalms.[8]

Had the work been accepted as Alfred's earlier than the mid-twentieth century, it would have had a happier editorial history. The standard edition, by James W. Bright and Robert L. Ramsay, was completed in 1907 and suffers many deficiencies, especially lack of a useful introduction or notes.[9] Their text, according to J. H. G. Grattan, is little more than an imitation of the edition first undertaken by Thorpe in 1835.[10] A new and much-needed edition is now in preparation.[11]

Authorship

The *Paris Psalter* does not contain a preface identifying Alfred's contribution, nor is the work discussed in other translations by the king. William of Malmesbury alone claimed that Alfred translated the first fifty psalms and that the king was working on the translation when he died.[12] Some corroboration of William's remarks appears in the *Life* of Alfred by Asser, who notes that Alfred was especially devoted to the psalter. From his youth he learned the psalms and collected them with other prayers into a book "which he kept with him day and night"; the king also participated "in certain psalms and prayers" in both the day and night offices.[13] It was only in 1885 that Wülker suggested that the *Paris Psalter* contained the text of the psalms that William had attributed to Alfred,[14] a suggestion developed by J. Wichmann a few years later.[15] The suggestion was not entirely dismissed,[16] but little more was made of it until 1950, when J. I.'A. Bromwich reopened the question.[17] Thereafter, at least a few scholars considered the possibility of Alfred's authorship to be good.[18]

However, it was not until Janet M. Bately's 1981 study of the language of the text that Alfred's authorship of the prose psalms was established beyond reasonable doubt. Bately demonstrated that the *Soliloquies*, the *Consolation of Philosophy*, and the *Pastoral Care* are by one author, Alfred, and that the prose psalms share with those translations lexical and stylistic features that are uncharacteristic of other prose texts of this period.[19] The link between the prose psalms and other translations offers new opportunities for study of Alfred's language and of the images and themes that dominate his work. However, as a look at the tradition of psalter study in the early Middle Ages will attest, the psalms present an unusual set of questions for critical inquiry, very different from those raised by philosophical and theological speculation or by pastoral advice. Indeed, the psalms are devotional texts of great theological and intellectual complexity and do not lend themselves easily to generalization.

The Latin Source: The Book of Psalms

The Book of Psalms is one of the most diverse and complex in the Bible, said to be the "most heterogeneous" because it is a "welding together of a sequence of one hundred and fifty lyrics, greatly varying in length, under the pressure of the times and customs that have embodied them into Hebrew and Christian liturgies."[20] They encompass divergent modes and moods, alternating supplication with complaint, celebration with lament, and frequently switching from one to the other within a few lines; their subject matter encompasses petitions for pardon, lamentations of persecution, and praise. It is certain that the psalms were set to music, and this would explain the patterns of repetition that are characteristic of their style. According to T. R. Henn, "Too many of the psalms seem to follow a kind of formula" in which the poet laments his misfortunes and the strength of his enemies, and "asserts his own righteousness, or his repentance, and calls for God's vengeance upon his enemies."[21] But they are varied, rich, and individual texts which are not easily comprehended as a single work of literature.

The problems posed by the variety of the psalms themselves were compounded in Alfred's time by the lack of a single, standard psalter text. In the early medieval period four kinds of psalter text, in addition to the original Hebrew and the Greek (or Septuagint) texts, were available: the Old Latin, a group of texts translated from the Greek, unknown in early England; the "Roman" psalter, considered the first revision of an Old Latin text (and still used in St. Peter's in Rome); the "Gallican," a thorough revision of the Old Latin by Jerome, used in Gaul; and the "Hebrew," a direct translation from the Hebrew psalter, studied in English monasteries but not used in church service.

The Roman psalter is thought to be the text brought by Augustine to Canterbury from Rome at the command of Gregory the Great in 597. At this time the Gallican psalter was popular in Ireland,[22] and, owing to Ireland's great influence on early English Christianity, was also used subsequently in England.[23] Both versions were available to the author of Alfred's source, since his text sometimes takes readings from the Gallican text; however, it was not until after the monastic reforms of the mid-tenth century that the Roman was replaced by the Gallican psalter.[24] Alfred's translation, the poetic translation of psalms 51–150 in the same manuscript, and additional Old English renditions of the psalms all derive from the Roman text.[25]

Exegesis and the psalter.   The psalms embody literary and cultural traditions specific to Judaism; when these poems were transposed into a Christian context, or "Christianized," many discrepancies and contradictions between Christian and Hebraic cultures had to be explained.[26] Attempts to reconcile these discrepancies eventually produced a vast body of exegetical commentary which sought to resolve literal contradictions and inconsistencies by recourse to figurative argument and explication. Commentaries distinguished between literal interpretation and other levels of understanding, reconciled the differences that existed on those levels, and thereby found common ground for Old and New Testament truths. Interpreted allegorically, the Old Testament psalms were understood to contain prophecies concerning Christ, to correspond to events in the life of Christ, and to pertain to the moral life of every Christian.

Allegorical exegesis, the chief method of interpreting texts in the Middle Ages, derives from traditions of classical antiquity. In the first half of the first century after Christ the Hellenized Jewish commentator, Philo Judaeus of Alexandria, a follower of the Greek commentators who allegorized Homer, found philosophical meanings in Scripture. As Beryl Smalley notes, such commentary is apologetic; it gives the author an opportunity to reconcile his own philosophy with that of a source which contradicts or denies it.[27] The objective of allegorical commentary was to establish a difference between the letter, or surface meaning of a text, and its spirit, or inner meaning: discrepancies might exist on the literal level, showing Scripture in conflict with Platonism, but these differences could be explained when harmonies were discovered on higher levels. When a text as holy and ancient as the psalms stood outside the writer's own traditions and beliefs, it had to be incorporated into the writer's system of thought—in this case, into the Christian perspective.

All great Christian writers—Augustine, Cassiodorus, Gregory, Ambrose, and others—used the allegorical method. However, they were not uniform in their purposes and approaches. Two schools differing in method are now identified. Followers of the Alexandrian school concerned themselves with the mysteries of the text and used allegory for speculation. The second school, the Antiochene, was formed in reaction to the mystical emphasis of the Alexandrian; it concentrated on the literal and historical truth of Old Testament prophecies, especially as seen in the psalms, rather than on speculative interpretation. A prominent member of the Antiochene school, which was by far the less influential of the two in the Western Church, was Theodore of Mopsuestia (d. 428); his commentary on the psalms greatly influenced King Alfred's sources.[28]

After the Greek exegetes, the first systematic interpretation of the psalms was Augustine's (d. 430). He imposed a design on the psalms which required that they be interpreted collectively, as parts of a single, overarching concept—the spiritual history of the Christian exiled from the City of God to Babylon and struggling to return to his true home.[29] In the sixth century Cassiodorus sought to make the interpretation of the psalms more rigid and scientific; he was the first to find in them grammatical and rhetorical figures derived from classical antiquity. To the objection that Hebrew poetry could not be expected to contain such tropes, Cassiodorus replied that they were implicit in the poems, just as wine is "implicitly present in the grape."[30]

However different their emphases, early medieval commentaries were alike in that they sought to explicate the psalms by constructing an interpretative framework and providing a preface to each psalm as a foundation for its explication. Each psalm thus acquired an introduction that explained its setting and situation as well as the identity of its speaking voice. By the third century the psalms were admitted to liturgical usage, and the psalter was considered "in its entirety as a prophetical book, fulfilled in Christ"; the psalms were "interpreted as comprising the voice of Christ addressing his prayer to the Father," and later came to be seen as the voice of the Church.[31] Thus, the psalms became an integral part of the divine office; by the early Middle Ages they had become a chief form of prayer in monasteries and the most commonly used form of private prayer among the educated nobility.

Exegesis in Alfred's time: the psalter glosses. The most common treatment of the psalms in Anglo-Saxon England was not commentary but glossing, not an interpretation of the text but a verbatim, word-by-word translation into Old English.[32] Fourteen glossed psalters survive from Anglo-Saxon England, six from the period of 975–1075, four of these from Winchester. Included among them is the second manuscript of the prose introductions in the Old English psalter.[33]

Psalters were glossed not because they were obscure—although the exegetical tradition shows that explication was essential—but because this form of translation of Latin was a very useful schoolroom exercise. The earliest Old English texts include psalter glosses known as the *Blickling Glosses*, written in Latin, in an eighth-century hand, with vernacular glosses from the ninth and second half of the tenth centuries.[34] Another important text is the *Vespasian Psalter*, with a Latin text of the eighth century and a ninth-century gloss.[35]

The tradition of glossing is one of the oldest and most continuous schoolroom activities of medieval England. The psalters preserve linguistic forms that had ceased to be used by Alfred's time, and for many scholars the chief value of glosses continues to be linguistic. In studies of Old English vocabulary by Hans Schabram,[36] Franz Wenisch, and others[37] the glosses are helping scholars date and localize these and other texts.

Alfred's Translation of the Psalms: The Introductions

Alfred's text is neither a commentary nor a gloss but a translation and paraphrase, with many changes from the Latin to the Old English; each psalm is accompanied (or was in the original version) by a brief preface. Scholars traditionally refer to the "introductions" to these psalms, but they are "introductions" in a medieval rather than a modern sense; while they explain the purpose and applications of the psalms, they also present the "guiding idea or theme." In Latin translations of the psalter each psalm was usually accompanied by a biblical *titulus*, a heading which often indicated "the circumstances of its composition, the occasion for which it was meant to be sung, or its author."[38]

The Old English introductions contain such information, but, more important still, contain an *argumentum* which explains the concept or theme of the psalm. Patrick P. O'Neill illustrates this method with the introduction to Psalm 6, which assigns its theme of suffering and sickness to four speakers or personae:

1. David sang this sixth psalm about his infirmity and about his sufferings, and also concerning the terror of judgment on Judgment Day;

2. and likewise does each one of those who sing it;

3. and likewise did Christ, when he was on earth: he sang it about his sufferings;

4. and also Ezechias about his illness.[39]

This four-level interpretation is typical of medieval commentaries, but the divisions are not. The first three levels in this example are standard: the historical level, which applies to David; the moral or tropological, which applies to any man who, like David, sings this psalm; and the mystical or Christological, which applies to Christ. The Old English then adds a further historical application, to Ezechias in this case, and in other cases to other Old Testament figures who lived after David. This fourth level departs from the pattern adhered to by Augustine and others, wherein the fourth level was traditionally an anagogical interpretation (that is, pertaining to the soul).[40]

The fourth level seen in the *Paris Psalter* seems to derive from Theodore of Mopsuestia, whose literal approach to interpreting the psalms was known in early Ireland.[41] The author of the commentary known to Alfred is believed to have derived his material "from an Irish plan for psalm commentaries."[42] He borrowed the exegetical matter to be used in his scheme from many sources, including a text once attributed to the Venerable Bede (d. 735) and known as *In Psalmorum Librum Exegesis*. This source contained three parts and provided for a threefold rather than fourfold scheme for interpreting each psalm: for an application either to David or to an Old Testament figure after him; then a mystical level; and finally a moral or mystical level. The commentator whom Alfred followed evidently attempted to devise a fourfold scheme from his three-level source but did not always succeed. Sometimes he omitted the fourth level, but more often he doubled the historical level, applying the psalm both to David and to someone who lived after David.

Either Alfred or the author of his source commentary exercised great ingenuity, conflating sources and methods in order to produce a consistent commentary. We cannot survey his achievement comprehensively, but his techniques and his purposes become clear through even a small sample of the psalms as Alfred translated them. Alfred's psalter cannot be discussed authoritatively until the psalms are reedited and their relationship to the Latin tradition is better understood. But clearly the author remained independent of his sources at many points, deviating from the Irish order of levels of interpretation, departing from the Roman psalter for Gallican psalter readings at some points, and modifying them to fit his own interpretative scheme. He changed his method as he worked, using no fixed order of the levels of interpretation for the first fourteen psalms before settling into a fixed approach. His work, as translated in the introductions to the Old English prose psalms, represents an original and skillful achievement in psalter study.

Alfred's Translation of the Psalms

The introductions to the first fifty psalms in the *Paris Psalter* differ from all known exegetical traditions. O'Neill's study of the introductions clearly establishes that they were written by the translator of the first fifty psalms, Alfred. But Alfred himself could not have known Scripture well enough to have single-handedly manipulated complex exegetical traditions. We may assume that his helpers translated the Latin commentaries for him and assisted the king in harmonizing his translation of each psalm with an appropriate introduction devised by Alfred. Thus, the prose psalms form a coherent text; as O'Neill comments, the author saw to it that "all information and details included in his introductions were in harmony, both with each other and with the general theme of the first historical, Davidic clause."[43]

The significance of Alfred's accomplishment will be apparent in a survey of the prose psalms and the alterations made as he translated and paraphrased the Roman text. Two major kinds of change will be discussed. The first pertains to matters of interpretation that show the author to be somewhat at variance with the Western exegetical tradition he could have been expected to follow. The second involves matters of language and style that modify the psalms and show the author's desire to include new material either for clarification or for stylistic effect. These additions, as we might expect, often reveal a kinship between the prose psalms of the *Paris Psalter* and Alfred's other translations.

Alfred's interpretative adaptations. The standard approach to the psalms was to understand all psalms as psalms of David, but to interpret many of them as utterances of Christ. A commentary such as Augustine's *Enarrations on the Psalms* almost invariably identified the speaker as Christ, even when the text did not warrant this belief.[44] The author of the introductions, however, did not always assume that Christ was the persona of the text; instead, he favored literal and historical interpretations, so that in his scheme many psalms are spoken by David, applied to the Davidic or post-Davidic era, and given literal and historical meaning.

The translator took this approach to Psalms 8, 18, and 44.[45] In Psalm 8, a hymn in praise of God's goodness ("O Lord, our Lord, how majestic is your name over all the earth"), which Augustine understood as being spoken by the faithful, the translator added, "He said, O Lord, our God," thus making it clear that the text is spoken by David.[46] Psalm 18, which begins "The heavens are telling the glory of God," the translator saw as David's prophecy of Christ's coming; for Augustine the psalm referred to the Evangelists.[47] The translator elsewhere stressed his literal interest in the text, adding, for example, "said David," to Psalm 11:7.

Psalm 44 defied strict explication on the historical level. The translator added comments that invest the text with allegorical import. When he translated "My tongue is very like the feather of the most ready writer," he adds, "that is, Christ, who is the word and tongue of God the Father, through Him are all things made" (44:2; p. 105). Again, after "Gird your sword upon your thigh," he added, "that is, spiritual teaching, which is in the Gospel; it is sharper than any sword" (44:4; p. 105). Both allegories, that of the pen and that of the sword, correspond to Augustine's interpretations.[48] Commenting on verse 7, which warns that "the people fall under you," the translator noted "that is either that they fall in confession or in hell." To verses 10–12 and 16 of this psalm he added extensive allegorical information concerning the spices and perfumes mentioned by the psalmist (44:7, 10–12, 16, pp. 105–7). Therefore, although the translator exercised a preference for the historical level of the psalms, he knew that at some points it was essential to admit allegorical explication into his text so that its meaning would be clear. Certainly his focus on the literal and historical level was a very conservative one, admitting as little ambiguity as possible, presenting the simplest interpretation of the text, and producing a clear translation of the psalms.

Sometimes his method avoided difficulties that the Christological focus posed for more traditional commentators. Psalm 21, which begins "My God, my God, why have you foresaken me?" is a case in point. These words, of course, were identified as those spoken by Christ on the cross shortly before his death. However, one phrase in the Latin text—"verba delictorum meorum" (the words of my sins)—naturally did not fit this context. Augustine suggested that these words belong to the "old man" whose sins Christ bore, the "old self" of sin crucified with Christ so that the "new man" of grace could be born.[49] The Old English translation establishes that these words are not those of Christ: "I call to you day and night, and confess my sins, and lament my misfortunes, and you do not hear it [my call]" (21:2, p. 43). Even though the introduction to this psalm identifies three speakers—David, every man, and Christ—the words that confess sins clearly cannot be Christ's but instead belong to David and mortal men. But sometimes the same tendency strains the obvious implication of the text. Augustine and other commentators interpreted the words of Psalm 21 as Christ's: "They have pierced my hands and feet, and they have numbered all my bones." But the translator, contradicting this interpretation, added, "That is, my might"; thus, the speaker cannot be Christ (21:15; p. 45).

Language and style. Many psalms show the translator's attempts to clarify the text for his readers by adding new transitions between verses as well as by establishing allegorical interpretations.[50] Psalms 2, 3, and 9, among others, are cases in point. Psalm 2:2 ("Why do the nations rage") describes "noblemen" scheming against God and wishing to throw off the yoke of David's just rule; as a transition between their utterance and the next verse—"For God who is in heaven derides them, and the Lord confounds them"—the translator wrote, " 'What avails their talk,' said the prophet, 'though they speak in this manner?' " (2:3–4; pp. 2–3).

The translator also supplied narrative connectors in Psalm 3. "Many say to my spirit that it has no protection from its God," the speaker laments. To this the translator added, "But it is not as they say" (3:2; p. 4). To verse 5 of this psalm, which ends, "Arise, O Lord, and make me safe," the translator added, "For you are my God." Similar transitions are created in Psalm 14:2, which begins, "Lord, who shall sojourn in your tent?" After this question, the translator observed, "The Lord answered the mind of the prophet through the inspiration of the Holy Spirit, and the wise prophet said, 'I know, nevertheless I ask, who dwells there.' " The text then continues with the answer, "He who enters without blemish" (14:2; pp. 26–27).

Psalm 22 ("The Lord is my shepherd") is another that shows the translator adding connectives that clarify. To the phrase, "your rod and your staff comforted me" (v. 5), he added a standard exegetical note, "that is, your correction and afterwards your consolation." To verse 2, "And turned my mood," the translator added "from sorrow to joy." This addition is not so much exegesis, as David C. Fowler says, as it is "merely an expansion for the purpose of clarification." Likewise, at Psalm 47:6 the translator explained the location of Tarsus, an addition that recalls the historical information that Alfred incorporated into the *Consolation of Philosophy*. Psalm 22:7 also shows the translator to have ingeniously explicated an error in his exemplar. Where the Latin reads, "My cup overflows," the copy before the translator wrongly read *populum* (folk) instead of *poculum*; the Old English reads, "How splendid is your people now, that each day they feast."[51]

Throughout the psalms the translator strove to create unity, to eliminate contradiction, discontinuity, and other possible stumbling blocks; he attempted a coherent, smooth, and, above all, logical translation—a thorough revision of the lyricism of the Latin into discourse. He minimized the disjunction of the psalms, their sudden changes from moods of joy to despair, by shaping each into a coherent syntactical unit. The addition of explanatory information was one way of minimizing disjunction. Another means, less drastic but equally effective, was to insert connecting words. In Psalm 4, for example, which rebukes those who do wrong to the speaker and then offers assurances of God's help, the translator added transitions—"nevertheless," "that is," "but"—thus creating links that did not exist in his source (4.5, 8, 9; p. 6). In another example, Psalm 6:8, "and" links three separate verses: "The Lord has heard my weeping voice, *and* God has heard my entreaty, *and* the Lord accepts my prayer; "therefore" is added to the verse which follows in order to establish that the psalmist's successful entreaties put his enemies to shame (6:7–8; p. 10).

The translator also can be seen to have embroidered his text with alliteration and repetition of synonyms, embellishments which add to its beauty and increase its clarity. His most frequent technique was to translate a noun in the Latin into two words, frequently alliterating. These word pairs are ubiquitous—mind and soul, mind and heart, soul and body. The word pairs serve a variety of purposes. Some examples expand and clarify rather than alter the meaning. For "my soul," the translator wrote, "my soul and my mind" (6:2; p. 9); for the eyes which are enlightened in Psalm 18:7, the translator added "either of the mind or the body" (39). The heart that melts like wax in Psalm 21:12 has become "my heart and my mind" (44). The soul lifted up in Psalm 24:1 has become "my mind and my soul" (50).

Other pairs combine literal and figurative meanings, for example, the contrasting pair "either spiritual or physical" in the introduction to Psalm 12 (23). In Psalm 29:6 the speaker, before a sudden illness, proclaims "in [his] pride and in [his] security" that his prosperity will never change (62). Another example is Psalm 10:2, in which flight through the "mountains" of the Latin source becomes flight "over mountains and through deserts" (20). Such pairs may merely repeat the sense already established in the Latin and enlarge on it but may also alter the meaning. They not only clarify the text and enhance its beauty but also transform it.[52] However, the first word of the pair is usually a direct translation from the Latin, so that Alfred's respect for the literal level remained a paramount consideration.

At some points, the level of language in the *Paris Psalter* becomes ornate and the effects very elaborate. Psalm 29 and Psalm 37 offer particularly impressive examples. In Psalm 29:8 the speaker asks how his death and decay will profit the Lord. Not content with the straightforward version of the Latin ("What profit is there in my blood, in my going down into the pit?") the translator stresses decay in the grave: "Lord, how useful is my slaughter to you, or my destruction, or my corruption in the grave?" (62). The violence of this language is echoed in Psalm 37:6–8, where the medical metaphor reappears: "Because my body is full of carnal desires, there is no healing in my flesh; rather, I am prostrated, and crushed, and humiliated, and I wail and groan very greatly with [my] whole mind" (87). The elaboration of the medical metaphor imparts the force of Alfred's own idiom to the translation and no doubt was meant to render the text more familiar, more similar to the literature he already knew.

This survey of changes in the translation only begins to indicate the many points at which Alfred and his source commentaries departed from the Latin text. Such departures were bold, for this was the most sacred of all texts and surely the most important and difficult of all those Alfred translated. Yet, despite its differences from the Latin, the *Paris Psalter* is the most conservative of Alfred's translations: it adheres closely to the text except where explanation seems essential to the reader's comprehension; otherwise, the changes—for example, the connectives and word pairs—either promote the coherence of the text, establish a logic for it, or make it more beautiful.

Relation to Alfred's Other Works

Like Alfred's other translations, the *Paris Psalter* was to some extent a vehicle for themes and ideas reflective of his chief preoccupations. However, the psalms do not have the same public quality as Alfred's other translations. They lack the didactic additions and digressions characteristic of his other works, presumably because such additions would have been inappropriate to a translation of Scripture. In other translations Alfred's apparent additions serve instructional purposes: they explain unclear assertions or provide information with which his audience would have been unfamiliar. According to Bately, the psalms, too, were a teaching text. In the context of the monastic classroom, one of the chief purposes of the psalms was to teach language. Alfred may have intended the *Paris Psalter* for classroom use, but he surely intended to use it himself. In the preface to Wærferth's translation of Gregory's *Dialogi* Alfred (or one speaking in his person) says that he wished to read holy books so that "I might occasionally reflect in my mind on heavenly things amidst these earthly tribulations."[53] The *Psalter* would have served this meditational and devotional purpose admirably; many of Alfred's additions impart a pious, devout tone to the work.

The *Psalter* also contains additions characteristic of Alfred's thoughts about kingship, leadership, and education. Certain similarities among the *Psalter* and the *Consolation of Philosophy* and the *Pastoral Care* suggest that the psalms may postdate other works. We must give at least serious consideration to William of Malmesbury's statement that this was the last of Alfred's translations—not because it reveals a greater preoccupation with spiritual matters than does the *Soliloquies*, for example, but because it seems to have attracted thoughts characteristic of other translations. In the psalms these ideas appear in condensed form, and it may well be that Alfred was able to refer to them concisely because he had already expressed them more fully elsewhere.

Some of these similarities rest on shared themes; others depend on shared language (lexical and stylistic features), and these similarities establish the closest correspondences among Alfred's translations.[54] A reliable text of the *Paris Psalter* will enable us to examine the links between this text and the *Pastoral Care*, which contains many references to the psalms.[55] When translating the same psalm for two different texts, Alfred was not, of course, obliged to quote himself exactly the second time, although he sometimes did. Psalm 22:5 was translated identically in the *Paris Psalter* (47) and in the *Pastoral Care*.[56] But some translations are different, not only from one work to the next, but within the *Paris Psalter*. The Latin versions of two verses of Psalm 48 are identical but Alfred translated them differently (48:11 and 48:20; 116–17). In the *Psalter* he examined each psalm individually and explored its context on several interpretational levels; in the *Pastoral Care* the psalms were used differently, chiefly to illustrate steps in Gregory's arguments.

Among the themes that establish links between the *Paris Psalter* and other texts attributed to Alfred are penance and the need to confess. As we have seen, Alfred introduced these concepts into the *Consolation of Philosophy* and developed them in other translations where they were mentioned only briefly in the Latin. In the *Psalter* Alfred added many references to the confession of sins. In Psalm 5:5 (7), those who displease the Lord not only do unrighteous works but do not repent them (the same idea appears in 34:16; p. 77); the reference to "words of my sins" in Psalm 21:2 (43) becomes "confess my crimes." Psalm 31 incorporates the medical metaphor in which sins are compared to wounds and confession is compared to cleansing. One who has kept silent and has not confessed his sins finds that his body is weak and his strength faded (31:3; p. 67).

Kingship is another theme important to Alfred that links the *Psalter* to other translations. Alfred might well have seen in David, author of the psalms, an ideal king, an author and a teacher, and may have been aware of the parallels between his own royal office and David's, for David too was a besieged king and a teacher devoted to the love of knowledge. Psalm 46, about the triumph of the Maccabees over their enemies, both Jewish and Antiochian, might well have had an irresistible appeal to Alfred, especially with its concluding vision of "the ealdormen of the earth" subjugated to the God of Abraham (110–11).

An addition to Psalm 38 brings to mind Alfred's need for solitude, also discussed in the *Soliloquies*. In the Latin the psalmist asks for respite; in the translation he asks, "Grant me now, Lord, some period of happiness, before I go from here so that I shall no longer be" (38:16; p. 90). The introduction explains that the psalmist wished "that God give him some comfort and a period of happiness in this fleeting life before his end" (89). The word for "period of happiness"—*rothwil*—is unknown outside this text; it recalls the request in the preface to the *Soliloquies* for a fine dwelling place where one "may, both in winter and in summer, live pleasantly and in tranquillity" in order to contemplate the writings of the fathers.

Another concept discussed in both the *Soliloquies* and the *Consolation of Philosophy* is concern for the afterlife, a concern which emerges with force and clarity in Alfred's translation of Psalm 48. The introduction identifies this psalm as David's warning to all men "of his days and after his days" that they not raise themselves up because of their wealth nor forget that they cannot take their riches with them into eternity. At verse 6 the psalmist intones, "Hear now, those who trust in their own power and boast and glory in the greatness of their wealth." He then warns them that no one can redeem his brother from hell if the damned one did not do good works while he was alive. Therefore, one should redeem his soul while he lives; if he does not do so when alive, his brother will be neither willing nor able to redeem him when the unrepentant one has died (48:7–8; p. 115). The psalmist laments the paradox that nearly all men strive in this life without realizing that with their labor they are earning only more labor—that is, suffering—in eternity, the punishment for their immorality. Nor do men think of their own death when they see the wealthy die, or consider that the foolish and the stupid die with the wealthy, who must leave their prized possessions to others. Alfred's *Pastoral Care* expresses a similarly gloomy view of human nature.[57]

The warning against false trust in worldly riches evokes Boethius, of course, although it also belongs to many other texts. But the combination of this warning with the concern for the redemption of another's soul cannot fail to remind us of the conclusion to the *Soliloquies*, which also concerns this linkage of the living to the dead, and which also stresses that nothing can be done for the departed who squandered the opportunity to save their souls when alive. That concluding passage, too, was a warning against false confidence in earthly riches, deriving its moral from the parable of Lazarus and Dives. Alfred did not refer to these figures in his translation of this psalm, but Augustine named them in his commentary on the text.[58] Alfred's interpretation, therefore, conforms to traditional exegesis of the psalm, but his expansion of the text and his thoughts at the end of the *Soliloquies*—a portion of the text that Alfred did not derive from Augustine—seem of one piece.

Alfred also brought unity to the later verses of Psalm 48. He warned that men who have almost no comprehension of the good while they are in prosperity and power imitate and become like dumb animals (48:11; p. 116). In his translation of the *Consolation* Alfred encountered the same idea: that to neglect the good and pursue vice was to lose one's human nature and become like an animal.[59] The Boethian parallel becomes stronger in succeeding verses, especially those which warn against men who seek to please God and man with words rather than with deeds, and who are so far from doing good that they lack even the will to do good (48:12; p. 116).

In his translation of the *Consolation* Alfred stressed the idea that one could be saved if he willed to do good works, that the intention to carry out a good deed was as good as doing the deed itself.[60] The strong influence of the Boethian doctrine can be detected again in the final verse of Psalm 48. The Latin warns that man cannot abide in his wealth, for he will perish like the beasts; Alfred's translation declares that those who will not heed the warning of the psalm when they are "in wealth and in honor" (48:20; p. 117) imitate dumb animals and indeed become like them.

That Alfred chose this text as an occasion to repeat his views on the nature of power and worldly wealth should not surprise us. Power and wealth are themes that figure more strongly in those translations—of Augustine and Boethius—that he rendered more freely and enlarged more liberally with his own ideas. To find the same concepts in the psalms seems to stamp them with the unmistakable mark of Alfred's thinking. Yet it would be a mistake to conclude a survey of his translations by underscoring the similarity between his translation of the *Psalter* and his translations of other texts.

To comment on and to enlarge the texts of Gregory, Boethius, and Augustine was ambitious enough for Alfred. He used the works of these venerable authors as a pretext for expatiating on the concerns that were most important to him, adding his wisdom to their authority. As a result, when we read his translations we hear two voices rather than one, Alfred's along with the Latin author's. But for Alfred to have introduced his own concerns into the psalms was far bolder, not only because the exegetical traditions were complex and the allegorical method elaborate and very learned, but because the psalms were sacred texts, the Word of God. To adapt Scripture was, for Alfred, tantamount to joining his voice with the voice of ultimate authority. We cannot explain Alfred's paraphrase and interpretation of the Book of Psalms as an act of piety alone; his confidence in rewriting Scripture seems to have been inspired not only by devotion, but also by his awareness of a Davidic identity as a teacher and a leader, a king and a man of prayer.

Chapter Seven

King Alfred in His Literary Context

The study of King Alfred's translations leaves us with the desire to learn more about the author of these important works and with the need to assess his influence on subsequent ages. Our knowledge of Alfred the man is great compared to our knowledge of other Anglo-Saxon figures—for example, the poet Cynewulf, or the homilist Ælfric.[1] But the sources that preserve his history tell us little about Alfred as an author. Since we cannot precisely define his role in the translations attributed to him or determine the chronology of his works, we cannot draw conclusions about Alfred's development as a writer. Biographical criticism, which would use the facts of Alfred's life to illuminate his translations, is therefore impossible. But scholarly approaches not dependent on biographical data and chronology remain open to us, and through these avenues we can further explore Alfred's translations and assess his importance to English literature.

Interpreting Alfred's Canon

Much scholarship about Alfred's writing seeks to establish a pattern in his works, identifying key themes which demonstrate coherence in the canon and help us to rationalize his choice of texts for translation. Various paradigms could be employed to unify his works. For example, we could trace a progression from the *Pastoral Care*, with its practical advice, to the still practical but more introspective *Consolation of Philosophy*, to the theoretical and abstract *Soliloquies* of Augustine. If we place the *Paris Psalter* at the end of Alfred's canon, as some critics do, we can complete a paradigm of transition from worldly to spiritual concerns. We cannot, of course, be certain that Alfred's interest actually flowed in this progression from the external to the internal, from the worldly to the devout. That progression may simply be a pattern that we have established in the modern period and unconsciously superimposed upon Alfred's canon; what is more important, it depends on a chronology that cannot be established.

Another suggestion based on chronology arranges the *Pastoral Care*, the *Consolation*, and the *Soliloquies* as stages in the development of Alfred's idea of knowledge, from simple book-learning, or *scientia*, to the more profound concept of wisdom, or *sapientia*. In this scheme the translations are said to reflect Alfred's "personal and public commitment to the ideal of Christian wisdom." That transition may be "a chapter in spiritual biography that in all likelihood can never be written with certitude."[2] But, like other paradigms imposed on Alfred's translations, it is both satisfying to the student and useful to the teacher in unifying King Alfred's translations.

Alfred's concern with wisdom was not unique. Bately has argued that *sapientia*, or divine wisdom, was in his time the "be all and end all of education." Had Alfred followed a continental concept of a classical education, he would have concentrated on the trivium and quadrivium, studies which prepared for the analysis of Holy Scripture. But Bately believes that Alfred went beyond the goals of classical education and sought to instill in his followers a love of wisdom. "For Alfred, as for St. Augustine before him, wisdom is different from knowledge," she notes; the king linked wisdom and learning, but identified wisdom, "the loftiest of virtues," "not only with the highest good but with God." Wisdom, God's gift, is to be used in God's service; properly applied, Alfred claimed, wisdom will lead to spiritual and material rewards.[3] Alfred's interest in learning can thus be said to have had social as well as spiritual objectives.

Other attempts at establishing the coherence of Alfred's canon stress the political importance of his pervasive concern with wisdom. Loyn aptly suggests that "Alfred provided in his translations the ideological basis for the Christian kingship of England" and emphasized themes related to the governance of a Christian kingdom—"submission to lordship and legal authority, the place of Christianity in world history, and fortitude in face of secular disaster."[4] In choosing to translate works that discuss the use of power, Alfred gave his scholarly projects a particular focus: not only to increase literacy in his nation, but to increase the moral awareness and Christian consciousness of his followers.

As we seek the common ground shared by Alfred's translations, we need to remain aware of their remarkable dissimilarities and to ask ourselves how Alfred, working at a time when learning had declined, managed to shape a canon so rich and varied. Scholars frequently disagree about the rationale of Alfred's canon; several have attempted to identify the principles that might have directed his selection of texts for translation. Commenting on Alfred's list of translations, Keynes and Lapidge observe, "This list of books will seem a curious, even idiosyncratic, choice to have served as the basis for a programme of educational reform."[5] But Wallace-Hadrill claims that Alfred considered these books "most needful to know" because they were "the obvious books for his purpose of self-instruction and general instruction in the social role of Christianity."[6]

Another scholar praises Alfred's choices as more refined and sophisticated than the "practical and political ideological disputations and admonitions" of seventh- and eighth-century authors.[7] Still another commends his selection of "single great works" for translation instead of concentrating, as did his predecessors, on homiletic literature for instruction in the fundamental matters of Christian living.[8] Surely the spectrum of "ancient and ecclesiastical history, philosophy, theology, and doctrine" which we find in his translations presented a more formidable challenge to Alfred and his assistants than did homiletic texts. No one doubts that Alfred's greatness as a scholar lies in his attempt to popularize complex, sophisticated texts, to make "the scholarship of the Latin tradition available to readers who knew no Latin."[9]

However, all attempts to establish a coherence for Alfred's canon assume that he consciously chose certain texts in preference to others. It seems more likely that he merely translated those texts that were available or known to him. We cannot safely conclude that Alfred, simply because he did not translate Augustine's *De Civitate Dei*, did not know of this work—one of the most popular books in the early Middle Ages, as well as one of the longest, and hence an insurmountable task for the king and his helpers.[10] But at the same time it seems futile to attempt to create coherence and logic in what may have been a felicitous rather than a systematic series of choices. To translate the *Regula Pastoralis* or the Book of Psalms would make sense in any age; but to translate Augustine's *Soliloquia* would seem to be an unwarranted investment of time and trouble.

New Directions: Alfred's Literary Language

The themes and ideas that unify Alfred's canon will always be subject to revision and reinterpretation. But we should see them as the last, not the first, stages in productive research about King Alfred. Little is known about his literary idiom or about the antecedents to his revival of learning; only by tackling problems of Latin sources, manuscript traditions, and language can we obtain a clearer picture of the state of learning when Alfred came to power and a better estimation of his literary achievement. Recent trends in scholarship of King Alfred are dominated by two approaches. The first, analysis of Alfred's literary idiom and style, seeks to establish correspondences among his works on the basis of language rather than theme. The second, exploration of the historical context of Alfred's revival, takes into account manuscript production and other signs of literacy in pre-Alfredian England in an attempt to discover for whom and by whom books were written in the ninth century.

Studies of Alfred's language and style have never been completely out of fashion. But now that his canon has been defined, and certain works, such as the *Orosius*, eliminated from it, inquiries into Alfred's language have new significance. In recent years close analysis of syntax and vocabulary in his translations has revealed a pattern of choice, a conscious preference for one word or a group of words over others.[11] Consistent preference for one set of words or phrases in several texts can be taken to indicate common authorship or perhaps common training in language and translation shared by different authors.[12] Such evidence is not yet sufficient to enable us to claim that a "literary language" existed in Alfred's time—that is, a preferred vocabulary in the vernacular to provide coherence among translations from the Latin. Only later, in the tenth century, did a literary language emerge in Old English, and then under conditions far more favorable to the production and creation of texts.[13]

Our power to discuss Alfred's authorship in terms of style and vocabulary is rapidly increasing. And as the evidence from lexical studies mounts, we will find new merit in certain older studies of Alfred's style, which are rich in useful ideas. Two such studies deserve special attention. One is a close analysis of verbal structures by Bacquet; it has been called an "indispensable first step toward the literary appreciation of Old English prose."[14] The other is *Der Stil König Alfreds*, a detailed investigation of Alfred's style published by Borinski over fifty years ago; this book, unfortunately ignored in so much subsequent scholarship, is one of the most underrated and interesting of all studies in Old English prose.

New Directions: Alfred and the Ninth Century

Because studies of Alfred's language focus exclusively on the texts, they require the support of wider investigations into ninth-century literary history and the learned tradition of pre-Alfredian England. What resources were available to Alfred when he began his program of renewal? He would have derived some of his texts from English libraries and some from libraries abroad. Contact between England and the Continent in the ninth century was regular and productive; indeed, Alfred's own boyhood travels adequately testify to such intercourse. Without a history of such contact Alfred would have been hard pressed to request assistance from continental leaders, such as Archbishop Fulk, or to identify both scholars and manuscripts that could be imported to assist his program.[15]

Resources available to Alfred in English libraries, especially the libraries in Mercia, may have been considerable. Stenton argues for a vital Mercian literary tradition as a counterpart of Mercian political supremacy in the eighth and early ninth centuries, and claims that it was "highly probable" that four of Alfred's assistants named in the preface to the *Pastoral Care* came from Mercia and represented "a tradition of learning which had descended to his time without interruption from Mercian schools established in or before the eighth century."[16] The Mercian tradition was without doubt an important source for Alfred's revival, but the list of Mercian works proposed by one scholar is too extensive, and as yet no alternate list has been suggested.[17] The term "Mercian" remains a vague and unsatisfactory designation for texts not written by Alfred, but we cannot doubt that Mercia occupied a position of intellectual leadership when Alfred came to the throne.

There is other evidence to suggest that England was not as devoid of texts as Alfred's preface would indicate. One measure of literacy in the early medieval period, a time when few either wrote or read, is manuscript production, the analysis of the quality and number of books that were published.[18] In a recent study of Latin manuscripts of English origin dated to the ninth century, and originating in all parts of England, Jennifer Morrish effectively challenges Alfred's claim that learning was in sharp decline. Even the form of Alfred's preface (according to Morrish, more properly classified as a letter than as a preface) betrays scholarly traditions in the many learned commonplaces it borrows.[19] David Dumville is another who argues that manuscripts from the ninth century reflect a respectable level of scribal skill, which in turn suggests that some of the necessary apparatus of the learned world was available.[20]

However, a list of manuscripts written or owned in England to 1100 shows a decided decline in manuscript production after the eighth century and a rapid increase after the middle of the tenth, information which does more to confirm Alfred's statement about the collapse of learning rather than to contradict it.[21] Manuscripts of the ninth century unquestionably are fewer than those of either the eighth or the tenth centuries, but English libraries may nonetheless have been better equipped than Alfred realized. As our knowledge of ninth-century manuscripts increases, our estimation of English learning in the period before Alfred is likely to improve, but not necessarily at the expense of Alfred's reputation as one who restored a vanishing literary tradition.

New Directions: Alfred and the Tenth Century

Many scholars have exaggerated Alfred's improvements in the quality of intellectual life during his reign, but few have ventured to overstress his influence on subsequent decades. Beginning in the reign of King Edmund (939–46) English monastic life was reformed; especially during the reign of Edgar (959–75), new schools and new standards of learning were established.[22] Alfred's achievements seem to pale in comparison to the vast body of works by Ælfric and Wulfstan and the writings of other learned authors of the later period. According to Greenfield, "Alfred's immediate political heirs consolidated and expanded his territorial gains, but though they made gifts to the Church and were not hostile to learning, they did not advance his educational and cultural program."[23] Wrenn suggests that the "general falling away of the arts of vernacular writing which followed Alfred's successful efforts may be found in the fact that Alfred did not produce a revival or rekindling of the religious houses."[24] Gatch agrees that although Alfred did much to revive learning, "his reign had not been propitious for a monastic revival."[25]

While we cannot deny the contrast between the conditions of Alfred's reign and the state of learning enjoyed by the later writers, we should avoid deferring automatically to the neat divisions of Anglo-Saxon literary history without attempting to establish connections between these periods.[26] A revival of learning required more than texts: it also required schools to train readers and writers. Thus, rather than search for direct links between late ninth-century literature and texts written at the end of the tenth century, we should turn our attention to learned establishments with roots in the earlier period which, if they did not flourish before the tenth-century reform, at least sustained the activities essential to a learned tradition. One such center was the royal city of Winchester, a center of learning of great importance to Alfred and his successors and also to authors of the mid-tenth century and after.[27] As a way of measuring Alfred's impact on the tenth century, we may look briefly at the evidence of Winchester's indebtedness to Alfred.

Many believe Winchester's Old Minster to have been the king's chief scriptorium. This is an unproved assumption, often acknowledged as no more than a probability but sometimes seen as a very good one.[28] Given the prominence of the city, which was the largest of Alfred's fortified boroughs and also a major trading and administrative center,[29] we may expect that Winchester's monastic establishments were instrumental in carrying out Alfred's educational program.

The monastic establishments at Winchester were ancient by the tenth century. The kings of Wessex were sometimes crowned and usually buried at the Old Minster, which was built by King Cenwalh in 648. During Alfred's reign the city began to change: the borough's defenses were renewed (between 880 and 886), a rectilinear street grid, which Biddle takes to indicate a "deliberate policy of urban formation," was imposed over the settlement between 880 and 892, and about this same time appeared the first sign of commercial activity—the minting of coins.[30]

During Alfred's reign and shortly thereafter two important new foundations were laid at Winchester: those were for the New Minster and for Nunnaminster. This new construction must be linked to the revitalization of the urban settlement. Alfred himself planned the new church, but it was built by his son, Edward the Elder. Alfred, his wife Ealhswith, Edward the Elder, and his son Edward were buried in Winchester. (Alfred was buried in the Old Minster, and his body translated to the New Minster about 903.) Thus the city retained its traditional importance as a royal residence while acquiring new magnitude as an ecclesiastical center.

The growth and development of Winchester into an urban center under Alfred's guidance had bearing on the success of his educational reform. A great deal of evidence, enough to give rise to the designation "Winchester school," suggests that in the late ninth and early tenth centuries the city was an important center of learning, a place where books in both Latin and the vernacular were being reproduced. Paleographers, having examined styles of handwriting and techniques of bookmaking, link an important group of manuscripts to early Winchester scriptoria. These manuscripts include the *Pastoral Care* and translations generally dated to Alfred's reign, including the Old English *Orosius* and the *Anglo-Saxon Chronicle*.[31] According to Parkes, these manuscripts reveal a "pattern of standardization" which includes a new style of hand and a new method of book construction. These traits signal a "scribal discipline" similar to that seen on the Continent in the eighth and ninth centuries. The first signs of this discipline in England are in manuscripts linked to Winchester: these, it may be said, were harbingers of the revival.[32]

The use of continental methods at Winchester scriptoria has indirectly been traced to Alfred. Parkes believes that Grimbald, sent to Alfred by Archbishop Fulk of Reims, was instrumental in the transition from insular to continental styles which the manuscript evidence outlines; after Grimbald arrived in England, he is said to have been sent to Winchester. Grimbald's influence on Alfred's literary output is the subject of considerable speculation; some have suggested that he influenced the earliest version of the *Anglo-Saxon Chronicle* (found in the Parker manuscript) and more generally was responsible for Alfred's interest in historical texts.[33]

The connection between the king and Winchester depends on a secure dating of these Winchester manuscripts to Alfred's reign and the years immediately following. Most of the manuscripts are dated to the late ninth and early tenth centuries on the basis of their relationship to the Parker manuscript of the *Anglo-Saxon Chronicle*, which has usually been assigned to 891. However, Dumville has suggested that this date is too early, and that the Parker manuscript belongs to the first quarter of the tenth century rather than the end of the ninth.[34] We may eventually date these important Winchester texts a full generation after Alfred's death. But that would place them instead in the reign of Alfred's grandson, Æthelstan, who ruled from 924 to 939. Æthelstan was perhaps the only other English monarch of the period with intellectual interests comparable to Alfred's.

If, even in the light of the vast body of evidence from Winchester, we are unable to create a satisfactory picture of Alfred's literary environment, complete with scriptoria and schools, we should remember that the manuscript evidence may be limited by the remarkable, fluid circumstances in which Alfred worked. As we search for evidence linking Alfred's translations to Winchester and other prominent centers of learning, we should remember that he was an itinerant king, with many royal residences and, it follows, several monastic establishments to carry out his wishes that books be written and copied. It is possible that the king traveled with his own school, a regular group of translators, and even his own scribes.[35] Certainly Asser's descriptions of Alfred reading and listening to books "day and night" suggest that the king had something like a traveling school with him, and that, as he headquartered in various residences, he continued to read, listen to others read, and give dictation, always with the same few scribes.

Such provisional arrangements had to suffice for a king who fought battles, reorganized his army, and engaged in numerous avocations besides learning. Alfred could not have contemplated a "monastic reform" on the scale that King Edgar and his monks, Dunstan in particular, launched after 939; his nation was not at peace, and his followers were in the main too ill trained to support highly organized religious life. We have no sign that Alfred chose to make Winchester a reformed monastic center, or even that he considered such reformation, or could have considered it; instead, the city supplied him with one of his greatest needs—reliable scriptoria. Alfred's renewal of the city's defenses and his replanning of its streets have their counterpart in manuscripts written and illustrated in Winchester, and they are powerful evidence that the force of Alfred's revival did not perish with him.

New Directions: Alfred and the Twentieth Century

Improving our understanding of King Alfred in his own time also requires a new look at how we study his works today. The literary criticism of Old English texts has long belonged to a category described by Edward Said as "academic literary history," which has come to us from the nineteenth-century masters of classical philology and cultural history. The principles of this criticism, with its emphasis on linguistic study and knowledge of Latin and vernacular manuscript traditions, now form the backbone of Old English scholarship. Accompanying the criticism of the academy is another sort, more congenial to the classroom, which Said calls "appreciation and interpretation."[36] Such criticism may be academic, but its chief beneficiaries are the general audience that King Alfred has always attracted—nonspecialized, but keenly attentive to the words and deeds of a celebrated monarch.

Critics such as Said, however, are interested in another category of discussion, literary theory, manifest in today's plethora of "isms," from "structuralism" to "deconstructionism" and beyond. Little work with such theory has been done in Old English studies generally, and none in studies of Alfred. Yet some of the most important questions about Alfred's texts open themselves to such concepts. For example, scholars struggle to determine what is "original" in Alfred's translations, as opposed to what is taken directly from his sources. But what definition of originality applies here and how does it relate to the apparently unsolvable problem of distinguishing the king's words from those of his helpers? That these questions have gone unasked is the result of imposing a modern concept of authorship on Alfred's time, when the link between authorship and original creation had yet to become dominant. A new critical orientation can help us redefine our idea of authorship and reexamine Alfred's relationship to the texts and traditions which were reshaped under his influence.

Contemporary criticism also reminds us that texts are "a part of the social world, human life, and of course the historical moments in which they are located and interpreted."[37] As we survey the history of criticism of Alfred's translations, we discover that each age has created the Alfred it required. The Victorians saw him as a precedent for Queen Victoria and the values of empire. It might be said today that the resurgence of interest in Alfred owes something to the renaissance of humanism in the classroom; what better subject for such study than a philosopher-king, a scholar, and perhaps a poet?

The object of situating Alfred's texts in the critical theory as well as in the institutional values of our own day is not to deny the need for continued investigations along more traditional lines. One need not dread the day in which all manuscripts are catalogued, all sources discovered, all linguistic puzzles solved. At the same time, Alfred's writing has always compelled interest because it seems to speak directly to its readers. Today scholars of Alfred's prose can learn to use the constructs of recent critical theory to reexamine traditional concerns with the authorship, originality, voice, and unity of his texts, and to analyze certain political issues, such as the questions of power and authority that dominate some of his translations. Without lapsing into the linguistic decadence of some fashionable theoreticians, justly blamed for deliberately mixing critical discourse with the writing of fiction, any adventurous Anglo-Saxon scholar can use contemporary criticism to find new ways to read and understand Alfred's texts.[38] By doing so, we will enlarge the meaning of conclusions already reached through traditional scholarship. After all, each age previous to our own has been able to put the study of King Alfred on a new footing. As beneficiaries of so much learning, we have every reason to use the language and methods of our own time as the means of understanding anew the riches we have inherited.

Notes and References

All translations unless otherwise specified are the author's.

Chapter One

1. F. M. Stenton, *Anglo-Saxon England* (Oxford, 1971), 269–70.
2. For an introduction to King Alfred, see Simon Keynes and Michael Lapidge, *Alfred the Great* (New York, 1983), which also includes translations of Latin and Old English material.
3. See chapter 87 of *Asser's Life of King Alfred*, ed. William Henry Stevenson, in Keynes and Lapidge, *Alfred*, 99.
4. For references, see E. G. Stanley, "The Scholarly Recovery of the Significance of Anglo-Saxon Records in Prose and Verse: A New Bibliography," *Anglo-Saxon England* 9 (1981):223–62; see 227 n.13. The opera is by Donizetti.
5. C. Lloyd Engström, *The Millenary of Alfred the Great, Warrior and Saint, Scholar and King* (London: Longmans, 1901).
6. Beatrice Adelaide Lees, *Alfred the Great, the Truth Teller, Maker of England, 848–899* (New York: G. P. Putnam's, 1915). For a complete bibliography to 1972, see Stanley B. Greenfield and Fred C. Robinson, *A Bibliography of Publications on Old English Literature to the End of 1972* (Toronto, 1980), 311–13.
7. The millenary of Alfred's death was incorrectly identified as 1901. See William Henry Stevenson, "The Date of King Alfred's Death," *English Historical Review* 13 (1898):71–77.
8. Charles Plummer, *The Life and Times of Alfred the Great* (Oxford, 1902), 210.
9. Ibid., 6.
10. Victor Hastings, *Alfred the Great* (New York: Popular Library, 1969); the novel was based on a screenplay by James R. Webb and Ken Taylor for a motion picture of the same name, released by Metro-Goldwyn-Mayer.
11. Eleanor Shipley Duckett, *Alfred the Great* (Chicago, 1956); Alfred J. Mapp, Jr., *The Golden Dragon* (LaSalle, Ill., 1974).
12. See, for example, R. H. C. Davis, "Alfred the Great: Propaganda and Truth," *History* 56 (1971):169–82, and D. P. Kirby, "Asser and His Life of King Alfred," *Studia Celtica* 6 (1971):12–35.
13. Paul E. Szarmach, "The Meaning of Alfred's *Preface* to the *Pastoral Care*," *Mediaevalia* 6 (1982 for 1980):81.

14. See Keynes and Lapidge, *Alfred*, 44–48, on the cult of King Alfred, and E. G. Stanley, "The Glorification of Alfred King of Wessex," *Poetica* (Tokyo) 12 (1981):103–33.

15. Alfred's image in history is conveniently summarized by Dorothy Whitelock, "The Prose of Alfred's Reign," in *Continuations and Beginnings: Studies in Old English Literature*, ed. E. G. Stanley (London, 1966), 67–103.

16. The tale is probably a late tenth-century fabrication; for text and sources see Keynes and Lapidge, *Alfred*, 197–202.

17. O. S. Arngart, *The Proverbs of Alfred*, 2 vols., Skrifter utgivna av Kungl. Humanistiska Vetenskapssamfundet i Lund, 32 (Lund: C. W. K. Gleerup, 1942–55), and Helen Pennock South, *The Proverbs of Alfred* (New York: New York University Press, 1931).

18. Eric Gerald Stanley, ed., *The Owl and the Nightingale* (Manchester: Manchester University Press, 1972).

19. For relevant sections from the *Chronicle*, see Keynes and Lapidge, *Alfred*, 113–20, 275–92. See the translation and discussion of manuscripts by Dorothy Whitelock, ed., *English Historical Documents* (London, 1979), 145–261.

20. Whitelock, *Documents*, 123–24, vigorously refutes the "propaganda" thesis of R. H. C. Davis in "Alfred the Great"; see also Keynes and Lapidge, *Alfred*, 40–41.

21. For detailed and comprehensive background, see Stenton, *Anglo-Saxon England*, 239–76, and D. J. V. Fisher, *The Anglo-Saxon Age* (London, 1973), 215–34.

22. The survey which follows depends on the Introduction in Keynes and Lapidge, *Alfred*, 9–48.

23. For a detailed geography of Anglo-Saxon England, useful in tracing the division of territories, see David Hill, *An Atlas of Anglo-Saxon England* (Toronto: University of Toronto Press, 1981).

24. See Eric John, *Orbis Britanniae and Other Studies* (Leicester: Leicester University Press, 1966), 37–43, and Keynes and Lapidge, *Alfred*, 232 n.19.

25. See Janet L. Nelson, "The Problem of King Alfred's Royal Anointing," *Journal of Ecclesiastical History* 18 (1967):145–63; M. B. Parkes, "The Palaeography of the Parker Manuscript," *Anglo-Saxon England* 5 (1976):166.

26. See Fisher, *The Anglo-Saxon Age*, 218 and the general survey, 215–25.

27. For an overview of this activity, see David Hinton, *Alfred's Kingdom: Wessex and the South. 800–1500* (London, 1977).

28. See Philip Grierson, "Grimbald of St. Bertin's," *English Historical Review* 55 (1940):529–61, and Janet Bately, "Grimbald of St. Bertin's," *Medium Ævum* 35 (1966):1–10.

29. See Henry Sweet, *King Alfred's West-Saxon Version of Gregory's Pastoral Care* (London, 1871–72; reprint, 1958), 5.

30. See Keynes and Lapidge, *Alfred*, 294 n.4, for a confirmation of Alfred's claims.

31. Stenton, *Anglo-Saxon England*, 270.

32. Davis, "Alfred the Great," 169–82.

33. D. P. Kirby, *The Making of Early England* (London, 1967), 213.

34. See H. R. Loyn, *Anglo-Saxon England and the Norman Conquest* (London, 1962), 281.

35. See Whitelock, "Prose," 67–68; quoted from Keynes and Lapidge, *Alfred*, 123. The *Dialogues* are edited by Hans Hecht, *Bischof Wærferths von Worcester Übersetzung* (Darmstadt, 1965).

36. Quotations from chapters 22 and 25 of Asser's *Life*, in Keynes and Lapidge, *Alfred*, 74–76.

37. See Asser's discussion in the *Life*, in Keynes and Lapidge, *Alfred*, 88–90, 255–56 n.143.

38. Translated from Hecht, *Bischof Wærferths*, 1.

39. Translated from Sweet, *King Alfred's Version*, 7.

40. See Whitelock, "Prose," 69–70, and Whitelock, "William of Malmesbury on the Works of King Alfred," in *Medieval Literature and Civilization*, ed. D. A. Pearsall and R. A. Waldron (London, 1969), 78–93.

41. Thomas Miller, ed., *The Old English Version of Bede's Ecclesiastical History of the English People* (London, 1959–1963).

42. Günter Kotzor, ed., *Das altenglische Martyrologium* (Munich, 1981).

43. Janet Bately, ed., *The Old English Orosius* (London, 1980).

44. Edited in facsimile by Cyril E. Wright, *Bald's Leechbook* (Copenhagen, 1955).

45. On this method, see Janet M. Bately, "The Old English Orosius: The Question of Dictation," *Anglia* 84 (1966):255–304.

46. Kirby, *The Making*, 213–14.

Chapter Two

1. On the date, see Keynes and Lapidge, *Alfred*, 39, 163. The dating is uncertain; Whitelock, in *Documents*, 407, states that the code was published late in his reign.

2. The laws are edited by F. Liebermann, *Die Gesetze der Angelsachsen* (Aalen, 1960), 1:15–123.

3. Alfred's treaty with the Viking Guthrum, certainly no later than 890, an important legal document, is not a law code and will not be included in this survey; for a translation see Whitelock, *Documents*, 416–17.

4. Keynes and Lapidge, *Alfred*, 39.

5. For commentary, see Janet Bately, "King Alfred and the Old English Translation of Orosius," *Anglia* 88 (1970):453. For complete bibliographical information, see Greenfield and Robinson, *Bibliography*, 364–68.

6. See N. R. Ker, *Catalogue of Manuscripts Containing Anglo-Saxon*

(Oxford, 1957), 57–59, no. 39 (this is also the oldest manuscript of the *Anglo-Saxon Chronicle*).

7. Ibid., 443–47, no. 373. There is a facsimile by Peter Sawyer, *Textus Roffensis (Rochester Cathedral Library ms A.3.5)*, 2 vols., Early English Manuscripts in Facsimile 7 and 11 (Copenhagen: Rosenkilde and Bagger, 1957 and 1962); see vol. 1.

8. On the manuscript tradition, see Keynes and Lapidge, *Alfred*, 303–4, and Whitelock, *Documents*, 357–62.

9. Edited by Liebermann, *Die Gesetze*, 1:529–46.

10. For a full discussion of the laws, see Frederick Pollock and Frederick William Maitland, *The History of English Law before the Time of Edward I*, 2d ed., 2 vols. (Cambridge: Cambridge University Press, 1968).

11. For background and translations, see Whitelock, *Documents*, 391–407, and F. L. Attenborough, *The Laws of the Earliest English Kings* (New York, 1974).

12. See Mary P. Richards, "The Manuscript Contexts of the Old English Laws," in Paul E. Szarmach, ed., *Studies in Earlier Old English Prose* (Albany, 1986).

13. For a review of evidence concerning the sources of Alfred's laws, see Keynes and Lapidge, *Alfred*, 304–11.

14. Stenton, *Anglo-Saxon England*, 60, notes that Ethelberht's were the earliest laws written in a Germanic vernacular language.

15. Milton Haight Turk, ed., *The Legal Code of Ælfred the Great* (Boston, 1893), 45. Whitelock has doubts on this matter (*Documents*, 358).

16. For a good introduction to Anglo-Saxon law, see Whitelock, *Documents*, 362–69.

17. Christopher Brooke, *From Alfred to Henry III 871–1272* (New York: W. W. Norton, 1969), 45–46.

18. Kirby, *The Making*, 180.

19. Fisher, *The Anglo-Saxon Age*, 230.

20. Stenton, *Anglo-Saxon England*, 276.

21. See Patrick Wormald, *"Lex Scripta* and *Verbum Regis*: Legislation and Germanic Kingship, from Euric to Cnut," *Early Medieval Kingship*, ed. P. H. Sawyer and I. N. Wood (Leeds: University of Leeds, 1977), 105–38, esp. 132.

22. Turk (*Legal Code,* 47) suggests that Alfred added them because he was familiar with such headings from his translation of the *Pastoral Care*.

23. Still the best analysis of Alfred's prologue is that which introduces Turk's edition, *Legal Code*, 30–55.

24. This overview follows that of Turk, *Legal Code*, 30–31.

25. Attenborough, *Laws*, 34.

26. See Whitelock, *Documents*, 408–16, and Keynes and Lapidge, *Alfred*, 163–64.

27. See Paul Fournier, "Le *Liber ex lege Moysi* et les tendances bibliques du droit canonique irlandais," *Revue Celtique* 30 (1909):221–34.

28. This material is analyzed by Turk, *Legal Code*, 33–38.

29. As Whitelock notes (*Documents*, 408), the quotation is derived from Acts 15:29, not Matt. 7:12.

30. Quoted from Whitelock, *Documents*, 408.

31. Turk, *Legal Code*, 32.

32. Quoted from Whitelock, *Documents*, 408.

33. Translation based on Attenborough, *Laws*, 63; remaining references to the laws are given in the text (number of law followed by page number) and are taken from this edition.

34. This is the division in Attenborough, *Laws*, 62–93.

35. See Dorothy Whitelock, "Wulfstan's Authorship of Cnut's Laws," *English Historical Review* 70 (1955):72–85.

36. Attenborough, *Laws*, 85–93.

37. See Patrick Sims-Williams, "Thought, Word and Deed: An Irish Triad," *Ériu* 29 (1978):78–111, and Allen J. Frantzen, *The Literature of Penance in Anglo-Saxon England* (New Brunswick, N.J.: Rutgers University Press, 1983), 85–90.

38. The revisions are discussed in detail by Turk, *Legal Code*, 41–42; quote from 42.

39. Cf. Alfred's revision, in Attenborough, *Laws*, 87–91, to similar statutes in the laws of Ethelberht, 9–15.

40. Cf. Attenborough, *Laws*, Ethelberht 39–40, p. 9, to Alfred 46–46.1, p. 87.

41. Attenborough, *Laws*, 37–61.

42. Quoted from C. L. Wrenn, *A Study of Old English Literature* (New York, 1967), 197.

43. Turk, *Legal Code*, 44–45.

44. Translation after Attenborough, *Laws*, 37.

45. See Attenborough, *Laws*, Ine 45, p. 51, and Alfred 40–40.2, p. 83.

46. Turk, *Legal Code*, 33, calls Alfred's version an "imitation" of the rule in Scripture, "the sense being however quite new."

47. Loyn, *Anglo-Saxon England*, 215.

48. Translated by Whitelock, *Documents*, 146.

49. This case is persuasively argued by J. M. Wallace-Hadrill, *Early Germanic Kingship* (Oxford, 1971), 148–51.

Chapter Three

1. The standard edition is that of J.-P. Migne, *Liber Regulae Pastoralis*, *Patrologiae Cursus Completus*, Series Latina 77 (Paris, 1862):13–128.

2. See Henry Davis, trans., *St. Gregory the Great: Pastoral Care*, Ancient Christian Writers 11 (Westminster, Md.: Newman Press, 1950), 3–16, for an informative introduction to the text.

3. The Old English is edited, with a translation, by Henry Sweet, *King Alfred's West-Saxon Version of Gregory's Pastoral Care*; hereafter page references to this edition cited in parentheses in the text.

4. For background, see Greenfield and Robinson, *Bibliography*, 316–17.

5. Simeon Potter, extremely skeptical, believed that Alfred "was unqualified to do the work"; see "On the Relation of the OE Bede to Werferth's Gregory and to Alfred's Translations," *Věstník královské české společnosti nauk: Třída filosoficko-historicko-jazykozpytná 1930* (Prague, 1931), 1–76, see 55.

6. See Davis, *St. Gregory*, 244 n.41.

7. For a discussion of Alfred's treatment of the Latin, see William H. Brown, "Method and Style in the Old English *Pastoral Care*," *Journal of English and Germanic Philology* 68 (1969):666–84.

8. Sweet, *Pastoral Care*, 7.

9. Kenneth Sisam, "The Publication of Alfred's *Pastoral Care*," in *Studies in the History of Old English Literature* (Oxford, 1953), 140–47.

10. For a survey of manuscript evidence, see *The Pastoral Care*, ed. Ingvar Carlson, et al. (Stockholm, 1975–78).

11. London, British Library, Cotton Tiberius B.xi; and Oxford, Bodleian Library, Hatton 20, edited in facsimile by N. R. Ker, *The Pastoral Care* (Copenhagen, 1956).

12. Sisam, "The Publication," 142: the prefaces in the Hatton MS are added leaves, not part of the gathering on which the text itself begins.

13. See M. B. Parkes, "The Palaeography of the Parker Manuscript," 170.

14. See Ashley Crandell Amos, *Linguistic Means of Determining the Dates of Old English Literary Texts* (Cambridge, Mass.: Medieval Academy of America, 1980), 171–80, for variants from a passage of the preface from five manuscripts.

15. See Dorothy M. Horgan, "The Lexical and Syntactic Variants Shared by Two of the Later Manuscripts of King Alfred's Translation of Gregory's *Cura Pastoralis*," *Anglo-Saxon England* 9 (1981):213–21.

16. See Ker, *Pastoral Care*, 24–25.

17. See Richard W. Clement, "A Handlist of Manuscripts containing Gregory's *Regula Pastoralis*," *Manuscripta* 28 (1984):33–44.

18. For a description of the manuscript and dates, see E. A. Lowe, *Codices Latini Antiquiores*, pt. 6 (Oxford: Clarendon Press, 1953), no. 838.

19. See Richard W. Clement, "King Alfred and the Latin Manuscripts

of Gregory's *Regula Pastoralis*," *Journal of the Rocky Mountain Medieval and Renaissance Association* 6 (1985):1–13, and E. W. Westhoff, *Liber de Pastorali Cura* (1846, 2d. ed., 1860).

20. See C. D. Jeffery, "The Latin Texts Underlying the Old English *Gregory's Dialogues* and *Pastoral Care*," *Notes and Queries* 27 (1980):483–88.

21. For background, see F. H. Dudden, *Gregory the Great: His Place in History and Thought*, 2 vols. (London: Longmans, 1905), and Jeffrey Richards, *Consul of God: The Life and Times of Gregory the Great* (London: Routledge & Kegan Paul, 1980).

22. See Richards, *Consul*, 25–69; quotations from 57 and 54.

23. See Keynes and Lapidge, *Alfred*, 296 n.12.

24. Richards, *Consul*, 260.

25. See Wallace-Hadrill, *Early Germanic Kingship*, 73.

26. Davis, *St. Gregory*, 9–11, and Clement, "Handlist," 35.

27. See Rosamond McKitterick, *The Frankish Church and the Carolingian Reforms, 789–895* (London: Royal Historical Society, 1977), 88–90.

28. For a survey of this evidence, see Clement, "Handlist," 33–36.

29. Wallace-Hadrill, *Early Germanic Kingship*, 67, 136, and Richards, *Consul*, 67.

30. Wallace-Hadrill, *Early Germanic Kingship*, 144, and D. H. Green, *The Carolingian Lord* (Cambridge: Cambridge University Press, 1965), 326 ff.

31. Wallace-Hadrill, *Early Germanic Kingship*, 74.

32. Richards, *Consul*, 142.

33. For an edition, see Elliott van Kirk Dobbie, *The Anglo-Saxon Minor Poems* (New York, 1942; reprint 1968), 110; Keynes and Lapidge, *Alfred*, 126–7. For commentary, see Sisam, "The Publication," in *Studies*, 144–45.

34. See Francis P. Magoun, "King Alfred's Letter on Educational Policy According to the Cambridge Manuscripts," *Mediaeval Studies* 11 (1949):113–22, and "Some Notes on King Alfred's Circular Letter on Educational Policy Addressed to His Bishops," *Mediaeval Studies* 10 (1948):93–107.

35. T. A. Shippey, "Wealth and Wisdom in King Alfred's *Preface* to the Old English *Pastoral Care*," *English Historical Review* 94 (1979):346–55.

36. Ibid., 351–53.

37. See Szarmach, "The Meaning of Alfred's *Preface*."

38. See Bernard F. Huppé, "Alfred and Ælfric: A Study of Two Prefaces," *The Old English Homily and Its Backgrounds* (Albany, 1978), ed. Paul E. Szarmach and Bernard F. Huppé, 119–37.

39. Jennifer Morrish, "King Alfred's Letter," in Szarmach, *Studies*.

40. See Keynes and Lapidge, *Alfred*, 259 n.164.

41. See Brown, "Method and Style," 668 n.4, for a summary of critical views on this point.

42. See ibid., 667 n.2, for similar observations.

43. See Richard W. Clement, "The Production of the *Pastoral Care*," in Szarmach, *Studies*, for a detailed discussion.

44. This example taken from Brown, "Method and Style," 672. See also Brown, *A Syntax of King Alfred's "Pastoral Care"* (The Hague, 1970), 11–20.

45. Brown, "Method and Style," 678.

46. Noted by Davis, *St. Gregory*, 242 n.1.

47. Translation quoted from Davis, *St. Gregory*, 21.

48. On the medical metaphor in the literature of penance, see John T. McNeill, "Medicine for Sin as Prescribed in the Penitentials," *Church History* 1 (1932):14–26.

49. On the medieval tradition of the *visio Pauli*, see H. Theodore Silverstein, *Studies in the Apocalypse of St. Paul* (London: Christophers, 1935).

50. Gregory quotes himself from the *Moralia in Job*; see Davis, *St. Gregory*, 60, 248 n.41.

51. Wallace-Hadrill, *Early Germanic Kingship*, 138.

52. See Frantzen, *The Literature of Penance in Anglo-Saxon England*, for background on penitential traditions contemporary with Alfred.

53. See Clement, "Handlist," 35.

54. Davis, *St. Gregory*, 8.

55. On the manuscript tradition of the epilogue, see Dobbie, *Minor Poems*, cxii-xv; for the text, see 111–12.

56. Ibid., cxii.

57. Malcolm Godden, "Ælfric and the Vernacular Prose Tradition," in *The Old English Homily*, ed. Szarmach and Huppé, 103.

58. Sweet, *Pastoral Care*, ix.

59. Wrenn, *A Study*, 218.

60. Brown, "Style and Method," 684; in *A Syntax* (19) Brown comments that Alfred's "style is mediocre, the argument sometimes strained or muddled."

61. See remarks on Sweet's edition by Carlson, *Pastoral Care*, 1:21–23.

62. For further commentary, see Simeon Potter, "The Old English *Pastoral Care*," *Transactions of the Philological Society* (1947), 114–25, esp. 122–24; and C. L. Wrenn, "Standard Old English," *Transactions of the Philological Society* (1933):65–88, esp. 65.

63. Richard P. Wülker, *Grundriss zur Geschichte* (Leipzig, 1885); Johann Ernst Wülfing, *Die Syntax in den Werken Alfreds des Grossen*, 2 vols. (Bonn, 1894–1901); Gerhard Nickel, *Die Expanded Form in Altenglischen* (Neumünster: Wachholtz, 1966)

64. See Gustav Wack, *Über das Verhältnis von König Aelfreds Übersetzung der "Cura Pastoralis" zum Original* (Greifswald, 1889), and Albert Dewitz,

Untersuchungen über Alfreds des Grossen westsächsische Übersetzung der "Cura Pastoralis" Gregors und ihr Verhältnis zum Originale (Bunzlau, 1889).

65. Brown, "Method and Style" and *A Syntax*; Carlson, *Pastoral Care*, 1:9–12; Ludwig Borinski, *Der Stil König Alfreds* (Leipzig, 1934); Paul Bacquet, *La Structure de la phrase verbale à l'époque alfrédienne* (Paris, 1962).

66. See, for example, Potter, "On the Relation," 118–19, and Brown, "Method and Style" and *A Syntax*, 11–20.

67. Keynes and Lapidge, *Alfred*, chap. 25, 75–76.

Chapter Four

1. Quoted by E. K. Rand, *Founders of the Middle Ages*, 136, from Richard Morris, ed., *Chaucer's Translation of Boethius's "De Consolatione Philosophiae,"* Early English Text Society, Extra Series 5 (1868), ii.

2. For the Latin text, with a discussion of the manuscript tradition, see G. Weinberger, ed., *Anicii Manlii Severini Boethii Philosophiae Consolationis*, Corpus Scriptorum Ecclesiasticorum Latinorum 67 (Vienna: Hoelder-Pichler-Tempsky, 1934); see xiv–xxi for a list of 84 pre-eleventh-century manuscripts. Some 300 manuscripts date from the eleventh to fourteenth centuries; see Barnet Kottler, "The Vulgate Tradition of the *Consolatio Philosophiae* in the Fourteenth Century," *Mediaeval Studies* 17 (1955):209–14.

3. Jacqueline Beaumont, "The Latin Tradition of the *De Consolatione Philosophiae*," in Margaret Gibson, ed., *Boethius* (Oxford, 1981), 282.

4. See Diane K. Bolton, "The Study of the Consolation of Philosophy in Anglo-Saxon England," *Archives d'histoire doctrinale et littéraire du Moyen Âge* 44 (1977):33–78; see also Beaumont, "Latin Tradition," in Gibson, *Boethius*, 279–81.

5. For a survey of scholarship, see Greenfield and Robinson, *Bibliography*, 314–16.

6. The standard edition is by Walter John Sedgefield, ed., *King Alfred's Old English Version of Boethius, De Consolatione Philosophiae* (Oxford, 1899; reprint, Darmstadt, 1968).

7. For a description of manuscripts, see Ker, *Catalogue*, no. 167, 217; no. 305, 358.

8. See Kenneth Sisam, "The Authorship of the Verse Translation of Boethius's Metra," in *Studies*, 293–97.

9. For recent discussion, see Kevin S. Kiernan, *"Deor:* The Consolations of an Anglo-Saxon Boethius," *Neuphilologische Mitteilungen* 79 (1978):333–40.

10. See W. F. Bolton, "The Alfredian Boethius in Ælfric's *Lives of the Saints*, I" *Notes and Queries* 19 (1972):406–7.

11. Malcolm Godden, "King Alfred's Boethius," in Gibson, *Boethius*, 419–24, esp. 420; and Sedgefield, *King Alfred's*, xvii.

12. See Alastair Minnis, "Aspects of the Medieval French and English Traditions of the *De Consolatione Philosophiae*," in Gibson, *Boethius*, 312–61.

13. On the history of translations see Nigel F. Palmer, "Latin and Vernacular in the Northern European Tradition of the *De Consolatione Philosophiae*," ibid., 362–409.

14. A. Campbell, ed. and trans., *The Chronicle of Æthelweard* (London: Nelson, 1962), 51; translation from Keynes and Lapidge, *Alfred*, 191.

15. The list of books donated by Leofric is analyzed in *The Exeter Book of Old English Poetry*, ed. R. W. Chambers, Max Förster, and Robin Flower (London: P. Lund, Humphries, & Co., 1933), 18–30.

16. See N. E. S. A. Hamilton, ed., *Willelmi Malmesbiriensis Monachi De Gestis Pontificum Anglorum* (London, 1870), 177.

17. William Stubbs, ed., *Willelmi Malmesbiriensis Monachi De Gestis Regum Anglorum* (London, 1887–89), 1:133.

18. See Allan A. Metcalf, "On the Authorship and Originality of the *Meters of Boethius*," *Neuphilologische Mitteilungen* 71 (1970):185–87, and John W. Conlee, "A Note on Verse Composition in the *Meters of Boethius*," *Neuphilologische Mitteilungen* 71 (1970):576–85.

19. Henry Chadwick, *Boethius: The Consolations of Music, Logic, Theology and Philosophy* (Oxford: Oxford University Press, 1981), is an excellent survey of Boethius's life and works. See also Edmund Reiss, *Boethius* (Boston: G. K. Hall, 1982).

20. Anna Crabbe, "Literary Design in the *De Consolatione Philosophiae*," in Gibson, *Boethius*, 239–40, lists a wide range of sources.

21. My discussion is dependent on the summary offered by Richard Green in his translation, *The Consolation of Philosophy* (Indianapolis: Bobbs-Merrill, 1962), 121–30; quotation from 119.

22. Rand, *Founders*, 177.

23. For early arguments positing Alfred's dependence on Latin commentaries, see G. Schepss, "Zu König Alfreds Boethius," *Archiv für das Studium der neueren Sprachen und Literaturen* 94 (1895):149–60.

24. Whitelock, "The Prose," 82–83.

25. See M. B. Parkes, "A Note on MS Vatican, Bibl. Apost., lat. 3363," in Gibson, *Boethius*, 425–27.

26. See Whitelock, "William of Malmesbury," 89–90, and Pierre Courcelle, *La Consolation de Philosophie dans la tradition littéraire* (Paris: Études Augustiniennes, 1967), 241–97. The earliest commentaries are by Remigius (d. 908) and by an anonymous late ninth-century monk of St. Gall.

27. See Joseph S. Wittig, "King Alfred's *Boethius*," 183, where Wittig discusses the Latin Book 3, poem 9.

28. See J. M. Bately, "The Classical Additions in the Old English Orosius," *England Before the Conquest*, ed. Peter Clemoes and Kathleen Hughes (Cambridge: Cambridge University Press, 1971), 237–51.

29. References in the text to chapter and page are to Sedgefield, ed., *King Alfred's*.

30. This information was commonplace in Alfred's time. See Hans Sauer, "Die 72 Völker und Sprachen der Welt: Ein mittelalterlicher Topos in der Englischen Literatur," *Anglia* 101 (1983):29–48.

31. On the name changes, see F. Anne Payne, *King Alfred and Boethius* (Madison, Wis., 1968), 123–29.

32. The meters are edited by George Philip Krapp, *The Paris Psalter and the Meters of Boethius* (New York, 1932; reprint, 1970), 151–203.

33. Compare this passage to *King Alfred's Version of St. Augustine's Soliloquies* (Cambridge, Mass., 1969), ed. Thomas A. Carnicelli, 62, where anchors are again virtues which give man security.

34. For the tradition of the three divisions of men, see Keynes and Lapidge, *Alfred*, 298 n.6.

35. For commentary on this passage, see Brian S. Donaghey, "The Sources of King Alfred's Translation of Boethius's *De Consolatione Philosophiae*," *Anglia* 82 (1964):23–57; see 39–40.

36. Green, *The Consolation*, 41 n.12.

37. This passage is translated and discussed fully by Milton McC. Gatch, *Loyalties and Traditions: Man and His World in Old English Literature* (New York: Pegasus, 1971), 106–12.

38. Metcalf, "On the Authorship"; Conlee, "A Note"; see also Sisam, "The Verse Translation," in *Studies*, 293–7.

39. Stanley B. Greenfield, *A Critical History of Old English Literature* (New York, 1968), 187–88.

40. Wrenn, *A Study*, 194.

41. See the brief bibliography in Greenfield and Robinson, *Bibliography*, 247–48, and George K. Anderson, *The Literature of the Anglo-Saxons* (Princeton: Princeton University Press, 1949), 273–85.

42. See Greenfield, *A Critical History*, 187–88, for a sample comparison.

43. The prose and verse forms of the preface are printed in Bruce Mitchell and Fred C. Robinson, *A Guide to Old English*, rev. ed. (Toronto: Toronto University Press, 1982), 218–20.

44. Kurt Otten, *König Alfreds Boethius* (Tübingen, 1964), 280; for a recent discussion, see Whitney F. Bolton, "How Boethian is Alfred's *Boethius?*" in Szarmach, *Studies*.

45. See Anderson, *The Literature*, 287.

46. Olga Fischer, "A Comparative Study of Philosophical Terms in the Alfredian and Chaucerian Boethius," *Neophilologus* 63 (1979):622–39.

47. The best discussion of Alfred's style is Otten, *König Alfreds*, 211–38; Borinski, *Der Stil König Alfreds*, offers a complex and sophisticated full-length analysis.

48. Wrenn, *A Study*, 219–20.

49. See Godden, "King Alfred's," in Gibson, *Boethius*, 419.

50. Payne, *King Alfred*, 4.

51. Ibid., 4, 16–19, 42; for an overview of her thesis, see Milton McC. Gatch, "Beginnings Continued: A Decade of Studies of Old English Prose," *Anglo-Saxon England* 5 (1976):225–43, esp. 226–27.

52. Payne, *King Alfred*, 51.

53. Katherine Proppe, "King Alfred's *Consolation of Philosophy*," *Neuphilologische Mitteilungen* 74 (1973):635–48.

54. Gatch, *Loyalties*, 114, and Otten, *König Alfreds*, 60–70.

55. See B. J. Timmer, "Wyrd in Anglo-Saxon Prose and Poetry," *Neophilologus* 26 (1941):24–33, 213–28; reprint, *Essential Articles for the Study of Old English Poetry*, ed. Jess B. Bessinger and Stanley J. Kahrl (Hamden, Conn.: Archon, 1968), 124–58.

56. Otten, *König Alfreds*, 280–84, where he summarizes his conclusions in English.

57. Ibid., 35–49; see the English language summary, 282.

58. For additional commentary on Otten's argument, see Gatch, "Beginnings Continued," 226–27, and for analysis of the contrast between Alfred's eschatological thought and the teleological assumptions of Boethius, see Gatch, *Loyalties*, 107–12.

59. On Alfred's debt to penitential traditions, see chap. 3, n.48 and 52.

60. Wallace-Hadrill, *Early Germanic Kingship*, 146–47.

61. Ibid., 147.

Chapter Five

1. This idea was first suggested by Wülker, *Grundriss zur Geschichte*, par. 486.

2. See Ker, *Catalogue*, no. 216, 281–83.

3. Ker, *Catalogue*, no. 186, art. 9(g), 244; see Karl Jost, *Wulfstanstudien*, Swiss Studies in English 23 (Bern: A. Francke, 1950), 208, and (for text) H. Logeman, "Anglo-Saxonica Minora," *Anglia* 12 (1889):511–13.

4. For a recent study of the manuscript, see Kevin Kiernan, *Beowulf and the Beowulf Manuscript* (New Brunswick, N. J.: Rutgers University Press, 1981), esp. 70–85.

5. For editions, see Greenfield and Robinson, *Bibliography*, 313–14.

6. See Karl Jost, "Zur Textkritik der altenglischen Soliloquien-bearbeitung," *Beiblatt zur Anglia* 31 (1920):259–72, 280–90; 32 (1921):8–16.

7. Carnicelli, *King Alfred's*, 2.

8. Ibid., 97; hereafter page references to this edition cited in parentheses in the text.

9. Quoted from chap. 88 of Asser's *Life*, in Keynes and Lapidge, *Alfred*, 100.

10. Richard P. Wülker, "Über die angelsächsische Bearbeitung der Soliloquien Augustins," *Beiträge zur Geschichte der deutschen Sprache und Literatur* 4 (1877):101–31.

11. See Thomas O. Cockayne, "The Blooms," in *The Shrine* (London, 1864–70) and Frank G. Hubbard, "The Relation of the 'Blooms of King Alfred' to the Anglo-Saxon Translation of Boethius," *Modern Language Notes* 9 (1894):161–71.

12. Henry L. Hargrove, ed., *King Alfred's Old English Version of St. Augustine's Soliloquies* (New York, 1902), xxxiii.

13. For a discussion of this approach, see Janet M. Bately, "Lexical Evidence for the Authorship of the Prose Psalms in the Paris Psalter," *Anglo-Saxon England* 10 (1982):69–95.

14. See Carnicelli, *King Alfred's*, 24–40, for detailed comparisons.

15. See Carnicelli, *King Alfred's*, 38–40, for a survey of evidence of authorship; and Whitelock, "The Prose," 71–72.

16. The standard edition is J.-P. Migne, *Patrologiae Cursus Completus*, Series Latina 32 (Paris, 1861):869–904, a reprint of an earlier edition.

17. John H. S. Burleigh, *Augustine: Earlier Writings*, Library of Christian Classics 6 (Philadelphia: Westminster Press, 1953), 17–63.

18. E.g., see C. C. Starbuck, trans., "Augustine's *Soliloquies*," *Basic Writings of Saint Augustine*, ed. Whitney J. Oates, 2 vols. (New York: Random House, 1948), 1:258–97.

19. See Franz Römer, *Die handschriftliche Überlieferung der Werke des heiligen Augustinus, Band II.1–2: Grossbrittanien und Irland*, Österreichische Akademie der Wissenschaften, Phil.-hist. Klasse, Sitzungsberichte, 276, 281 (Vienna, 1972), pt. 1, 169–71; pt. 2, 314.

20. The following discussion is indebted to Peter Brown, *Augustine of Hippo* (Berkeley: University of California Press, 1969), esp. chaps. 10, 11; quotation from p. 123.

21. Quoted in Burleigh, *Augustine*, 17.

22. See Burleigh, *Augustine*, 19–20, and Brown, *Augustine*, 123.

23. Burleigh, *Augustine*, 19.

24. Ibid., 63.

25. Epistle 147, *De Videndo Deo*, Corpus Christianorum Series Latina 44.3 (Turnholt: Brepols, 1980): 274–331; trans. Sister Wilfrid Parsons, *Saint Augustine's Letters*, Fathers of the Church 20 (Washington, D. C.: Catholic University of America Press, 1953; reprint, 1965), 170–224.

26. See Carnicelli, *King Alfred's*, 28 and refs.

27. See Parsons, *Saint Augustine's Letters*, chaps. 2, 3, and 25–28.

28. The land was free from customary burdens called "public burdens," such as food-rent to the king, but not other obligations, such as maintaining bridges. See Keynes and Lapidge, *Alfred*, 308–9.

29. Burleigh, *Augustine*, 23.

30. See Asser's *Life*, in Keynes and Lapidge, *Alfred*, 75–76, chap. 24.

31. Quoted from Burleigh, *Augustine*, 25.

32. There is a careful analysis of this passage in Gatch, "King Alfred's Version of Augustine's *Soliloquia*," in Szarmach, *Studies*, 28–29.

33. This section of the manuscript is defective; large sections of the text discussing the virtues are missing. See Jost, cited in note 6.

34. Alfred's allusion to the "co-worker" in this passage is from 1 Cor. 3:9; see Hargrove, trans., *King Alfred's*, 19 n.2.

35. Burleigh, *Augustine*, 36.

36. For commentary on this passage, see Szarmach, "The Meaning," 73–75.

37. Carnicelli, *King Alfred's*, 28.

38. See Carnicelli, *King Alfred's*, 92, notes, for the proper sequence of the text.

39. This break is not indicated in Hargrove, trans., *King Alfred's*, 44.

40. The parable of Lazarus and Dives is found in Luke 16:19–31. On the source, see Carnicelli, *King Alfred's*, 106 n.95.9.

41. See Carnicelli, *King Alfred's*, 97 n.2.

42. E. T. Silk, "Boethius's *Consolatio Philosophiae* as a Sequel to Augustine's *Dialogues* and *Soliloquia*," *Harvard Theological Review* 32 (1939):19–39.

43. Quoted by E. K. Rand, *Founders of the Middle Ages*, 139.

44. See Anna Crabbe, "Literary Design in the *De Consolatione Philosophiae*," in Gibson, *Boethius*, 261.

45. See Brown, *Augustine*, 123.

46. See Whitelock, "The Prose," 80–86, for a comparison of the translations.

47. See Hubbard, "The Relation of the 'Blooms of King Alfred,' " 161–71.

48. Carnicelli, *King Alfred's*, 29–37, quotation from 32.

49. Both texts also "contain additions that show a thorough knowledge of the life and thinking of a king," according to Carnicelli, *King Alfred's*, 32.

50. Carnicelli prints four of these passages, *King Alfred's*, 30.

51. For the *Soliloquies* see Carnicelli, *King Alfred's*, 78, and, for the *Consolation*, see Sedgefield, ed., *King Alfred's*, 121.

52. Carnicelli, *King Alfred's*, 32 n.49.

53. F. Anne Payne suggests simultaneous translation in *King Alfred and Boethius*, 127.

54. Hargrove, ed., *King Alfred's*, xxx, xi.

55. Wrenn, *A Study*, 220–21.

56. Greenfield, *A Critical History*, 37.

57. Keynes and Lapidge list the sources, *Alfred*, 299 n.4.

58. Gatch, "King Alfred's," in Szarmach, *Studies*, 37.

59. Ruth Waterhouse, "Tone in Alfred's Version," in Szarmach, *Studies*, 79.

60. Potter's claim that the preface is complete notwithstanding; see Simeon Potter, "King Alfred's Last Preface," 28, and Carnicelli, *King Alfred's*, 1–2, nn.3–5, for a survey of opinion on the matter.

61. Gatch, "King Alfred's," in Szarmach, *Studies*, 25.

Chapter Six

1. See Greenfield and Robinson, *Bibliography*, 341–42.

2. For a description of the manuscript, see Ker, *Catalogue*, no. 367, 440–41. A facsimile of the text is edited by Bertram Colgrave, *The Paris Psalter* (Copenhagen, 1958).

3. For commentary on the metrical psalms, see Helen Bartlett, *The Metrical Division of the Paris Psalter* (Baltimore, 1896).

4. See Robert L. Ramsay, "The Latin Text of the Paris Psalter: A Collation and Some Conclusions," *American Journal of Philology* 41 (1920):147–76.

5. See Dobbie, ed., *The Anglo-Saxon Minor Poems*, 50, for a psalm quoted in the *Menologium*, lines 60–62; for the *Kentish Hymn*, 87–88; and for *Psalm 50*, 88–94.

6. This is London, British Library, Cotton Vitellius E.xviii, no. 224 in Ker's *Catalogue*, a psalter edited by James L. Rosier, *The Vitellius Psalter*, Cornell Studies in English 42 (Ithaca: Cornell University Press, 1962).

7. See Colgrave, *Psalter*, 16.

8. See Colgrave, *Psalter*, 1–15, for a description; compare Ker, *Catalogue*, 440.

9. James W. Bright and Robert L. Ramsay, eds., *Liber Psalmorum* (Boston, 1907).

10. J. H. G. Grattan, "On the Text of the Prose Portion of the *Paris Psalter*," *Modern Language Review* 4 (1909):185–89; Benjamin Thorpe, *Libri Psalmorum versio antiqua latina* (Oxford, 1835).

11. The text is being edited by Patrick P. O'Neill; I wish to thank Professor O'Neill for sharing his scholarship in unpublished form.

12. See William Stubbs, ed., *Willelmi Malmesbiriensis Monachi De Gestis Regum*, 1:132.

13. See the translation of Asser's *Life of King Alfred* by Keynes and Lapidge, *Alfred*, 75 (chap. 24), 91 (chap. 76) and 99 (chap. 88).

14. Wülker, *Grundriss zur Geschichte*, par. 500–501.

15. J. Wichmann, "König Ælfred's angelsächsische Übertragung der Psalmen I-LI Excl.," *Anglia* 11 (1889):39–96.

16. A. S. Cook, *Biblical Quotations in Old English Prose Writers* (London, 1898), xl.

17. J. I'A. Bromwich, "Who Was the Translator of the Prose Portion of the Paris Psalter?" in *The Early Cultures of North-West Europe*, ed. Cyril Fox and Bruce Dickins, (Cambridge, 1950), 289–303.

18. See, e.g., Whitelock, "The Prose," 94–95, and Greenfield, *A Critical History*, 38–39; less certain was Wrenn, *A Study*, 202.

19. Bately, "Lexical Evidence," 69–95, and "King Alfred," 454–56.

20. T. R. Henn, *The Bible as Literature* (New York: Oxford University Press, 1970), 123.

21. Henn, *The Bible*, 141, discusses the difficulties of reading the psalms as literature.

22. This form of the psalter is preserved in an early seventh-century Irish manuscript, the *Cathach of St. Columba*; see Martin McNamara, "Psalter Text and Psalter Study in the Early Irish Church," *Proceedings of the Royal Irish Academy* 73, sec. C (1973):201–98.

23. Celia Sisam and Kenneth Sisam, eds., *The Salisbury Psalter* (London, 1959), 47–48; see 48 for a list of manuscripts of the Roman and Gallican psalters of English provenance.

24. See K. Wildhagen, "Studien zum Psalterium Romanum in England," *Festschrift für Lorenz Morsbach*, ed. F. Holthausen and H. Spies (Halle: B. H. Spies, 1913), 417–72, and Sisams, *Salisbury Psalter*, 47–49.

25. Sisams, *Psalter*, 49. The other Old English texts are the *Kentish Hymn* and *Psalm 50*. They have been edited by Dobbie; see note 5 above. See also the Sisams' comments in Colgrave, *Psalter*, 15–16.

26. For further discussion of the "Christianizing" of the psalms, see Pierre Salmon, *The Breviary through the Centuries*, trans. Sister David Mary (Collegeville, Minn.: Liturgical Press, 1962), 153 n.158 and refs.

27. See Beryl Smalley, *The Study of the Bible in the Middle Ages* (Oxford: Basil Blackwell, 1952; reprint, Indiana: University of Notre Dame Press, 1964), 4.

28. This influence is especially interesting since Theodore's writings were condemned at the Council of Constantinople in 553. See Smalley, *The Bible*, 14–16.

29. My analysis is heavily indebted to Salmon, *Breviary*, 45–49.

30. See Ernst Robert Curtius, *European Literature and the Latin Middle Ages*, trans. Willard R. Trask (New York: Pantheon Books, 1953), 41.

31. See Salmon, *Breviary*, 43.

32. The first important study of this subject was Uno L. Lindelöf, *Studien zu altenglischen Psalterglossen*, Bonner Beiträge zur Anglistick 13 (Bonn: P. Hanstein, 1904).

33. London, British Library, Cotton Vitellius E.xviii; see Rosier, *Vitellius Psalter*, xii-xiii for a complete list of editions.

34. Henry Sweet, ed., *The Oldest English Texts*, Early English Text Society, Original Series 83 (London: Oxford University Press, 1885; reprint, 1966), 112–23; Richard Morris, ed., *The Blickling Homilies*, Early English Text Society, Original Series 58, 63, 73 (London, 1874–80; reprint, 1970), 251–63. See Ker, *Catalogue*, 266–67, no. 203.

35. See Sherman M. Kuhn, ed., *The Vespasian Psalter* (Ann Arbor: University of Michigan Press, 1965), and Sweet, *Oldest*, 183–401; Ker, *Catalogue*, 348, no. 287.

36. Han Schabram, *Superbia: Studien zum altenglischen Wortschatz, I* (Munich: Wilhelm Fink, 1965), 36–51.

37. Franz Wenisch, *Spezifisch anglisches Wortgut in den nord-humbrischen Interlinearglossierungen des Lukasevangeliums* (Heidelberg: Carl Winter, 1979); see index; Elmar Seebold, "Die AE. Entsprechungen von lat. *sapiens* und *prudens*," *Anglia* 92 (1974):291–333.

38. This terminology has recently been clarified by Patrick P. O'Neill, "The Old English Introductions to the Prose Psalms of the Paris Psalter," in *Eight Anglo-Saxon Studies*, ed. Joseph Wittig (Chapel Hill, 1981), 26.

39. Quoted from O'Neill, "Introductions," 26; all citations of the Old English translation are from Bright and Ramsay, eds., *Liber Psalmorum*.

40. Condensed from O'Neill, "Introductions," 27–28.

41. R. L. Ramsay, "Theodore of Mopsuestia in England and Ireland," *Zeitschrift für Celtische Philologie* 8 (1912):452–97.

42. See O'Neill, "Introductions," 27–31, for background.

43. O'Neill, "Introductions," 38.

44. Trans. A. Cleveland Coxe, *Expositions on the Book of Psalms*, Nicene and Post-Nicene Fathers of the Christian Church 8 (New York, 1888).

45. See J. D. Bruce, "The Anglo-Saxon Version of the Book of Psalms commonly known as the Paris Psalter," *Publications of the Modern Language Association* 9 (1894):43–164; see 67.

46. Bright and Ramsay, *Liber Psalmorum* (8:1; p.13); hereafter cited in parentheses in the text by psalm, verse, and page number. The editors number the psalms according to the manuscript, not according to the Vulgate.

47. See Coxe, *Expositions*, 54.

48. Ibid., 147–48.

49. Here Augustine refers to St. Paul, Romans 6:6. See Coxe, *Expositions*, 58 and notes.

50. The only detailed study of the translator's language available is John D. Tinkler, *Vocabulary and Syntax* (The Hague, 1971).

51. The Vulgate text is "calix." On the error, see David C. Fowler, *The Bible in Early English Literature* (Seattle: University of Washington Press, 1976), 94–95.

52. See Bately, *Literary Prose*, 14–15, on this combination of translation and commentary.

53. From Keynes and Lapidge, *Alfred*, 123.

54. See Bately, "Lexical Evidence," for lexical correspondences; the discussion by Bruce, "The Anglo-Saxon Version," 142–59, minimizes points of comparison, reflecting Bruce's conviction that the psalms were not Alfred's.

55. This question has been investigated by Bromwich, "Who Was the

Translator?" 297–300, Wichmann, "König Ælfred's," 71, 82–93, and Cook, *Biblical Quotations*, xi.

56. See Henry Sweet, ed. *King Alfred's Version*, 1:125.
57. Ibid., 239.
58. See Coxe, *Expositions*, 172.
59. See Sedgefield, ed., *King Alfred's Old English Version*, chap. 34.1, 58, chap. 37.3, 114; chap. 41.5, 146.
60. Ibid., chap. 36.8, 110.

Chapter Seven

1. See Daniel G. Calder, *Cynewulf*, Twayne's English Authors Series 327 (Boston, 1981); James Hurt, *Ælfric*, Twayne's English Authors Series 131 (Boston, 1977).
2. Szarmach, "The Meaning of Alfred's *Preface*, 77–80."
3. Bately, *Literary Prose*, 8, quoting Alfred's *Soliloquies*, ed. Carnicelli, 51.
4. Loyn, *Anglo-Saxon England*, 282.
5. Keynes and Lapidge, *Alfred*, 34.
6. Wallace-Hadrill, *Early Germanic Kingship*, 142.
7. Greenfield, *A Critical History*, 44.
8. See Peter Clemoes, "Late Old English Literature," *Tenth-Century Studies*, ed. David Parsons (London: Phillimore, 1975), 105.
9. See Malcolm Godden, "Ælfric and the Vernacular Prose Tradition," in Szarmach and Huppé, *Old English Homily*, 106.
10. See Jack D. A. Ogilvy, *Books Known to the English, 597–1066* (Cambridge, Mass.: Medieval Academy of America, 1967), and "Addenda et Corrigenda" to this work, *Mediaevalia* 7 (1984 for 1981):281–325.
11. Bately's work on Alfred's language is the most extensive; other important studies are those by O'Neill and Horgan (see Bibliography).
12. See Bately, "Lexical Evidence" and *Literary Prose*.
13. Helmut Gneuss, "The Origin of Standard Old English and Æthelwold's School at Winchester," *Anglo-Saxon England* 1 (1972):63–83.
14. Bacquet, *La Structure*; quotation from Carnicelli, *King Alfred's Version*, 24 n.44.
15. See Wallace-Hadrill, "The Franks and the English in the Ninth Century."
16. Stenton, *Anglo-Saxon England*, 270.
17. R. Vleeskruyer, *The Life of St. Chad: An Old English Homily* (Amsterdam: North-Holland, 1953), 38–62.
18. For background, see M. B. Parkes, "The Literacy of the Laity," in *Literature and Western Civilization: The Medieval World*, ed. David Daiches and Anthony K. Thorlby (London: Aldus, 1973), 555–77.
19. Morrish, "King Alfred's Letter," in Szarmach, *Studies*.

20. David N. Dumville, "English Libraries before 1066," *Insular Latin Studies*, ed. Michael Herren (Toronto: Pontifical Institute of Mediaeval Studies, 1981), 153–78.

21. Helmut Gneuss, "A Preliminary List of Manuscripts Written or Owned in England up to 1100," *Anglo-Saxon England* 9 (1981):1–60.

22. For an overview of the reform, see essays in *Tenth-Century Studies*, ed. David Parsons, especially D. H. Farmer, "The Progress of the Monastic Revival," and D. A. Bullough, "The Continental Background of the Reform."

23. Greenfield, *A Critical History*, 45.

24. Wrenn, *A Study*, 223.

25. Milton McC. Gatch, *Preaching and Theology in Anglo-Saxon England: Ælfric and Wulfstan* (Toronto: University of Toronto Press, 1977), 9.

26. See J. Armitage Robinson, *The Times of St. Dunstan* (Oxford: Clarendon Press, 1923), for an excellent discussion of pre-reform conditions.

27. For background and important discussions, see Martin Biddle, ed., *Winchester in the Early Middle Ages. An Edition and Discussion of the Winton Domesday*. Winchester Studies 1 (Oxford: Clarendon Press, 1976).

28. See Hinton, *Alfred's Kingdom*, 42; Linda L. Brownrigg, "Manuscripts Containing English Decoration 871–1066, Catalogued and Illustrated: A Review," *Anglo-Saxon England* 7 (1978):239–66; see 258.

29. Biddle, *Winchester*, 259.

30. Martin Biddle, "*Felix Urbs Withonia*: Winchester in the Age of Monastic Reform" in *Tenth-Century Studies*, ed. Parsons, 125–27; see also Biddle, *Winchester*, 277.

31. For a list of Winchester manuscripts, see Parkes, "The Palaeography," 156–63, and Dumville, "English Libraries," 168–69.

32. Parkes, "Palaeography," 158.

33. Ibid., 163–66. On the *Chronicle* text in the earliest manuscript, Cambridge, Corpus Christi College 173, see Ker, *Catalogue*, 57–59, no. 39.

34. Dumville, "English Libraries," 169.

35. I wish to thank Richard Clement for suggesting the concept of Alfred's traveling school.

36. Edward W. Said, *The World, the Text, and the Critic* (Cambridge: Harvard University Press, 1983), 1.

37. Ibid., 4.

38. For a critique of post-structuralism, see Frank Lentricchia, *After the New Criticism* (Chicago: University of Chicago Press, 1980).

Selected Bibliography

The primary sources include works by Alfred and other Old English texts important to studying Alfred's milieu. The list of secondary sources balances general works concerning Alfred and his time and specialized studies of specific works. Only a few of the latter studies are included in the bibliography; the notes to each chapter refer to several additional studies of each translation. For guides to further reading, consult the bibliographies compiled by Greenfield and Robinson, Keynes and Lapidge, and Berkhout.

PRIMARY SOURCES

Attenborough, F. L., ed. and trans. *The Laws of the Earliest English Kings.* Cambridge: Cambridge University Press, 1922; reprint, New York: AMS Press, 1974.

Bately, Janet, ed. *The Old English Orosius.* Early English Text Society, Extra Series 6. London: Oxford University Press, 1980.

Bright, James W., and Robert L. Ramsay, eds. *Liber Psalmorum: The West-Saxon Psalms, Being the Prose Portion, or the "First Fifty," of the so-called Paris Psalter.* Boston: D. C. Heath & Co., 1907.

Carlson, Ingvar, ed. *The Pastoral Care, Edited from British Library MS. Cotton Otho B.ii.* 2 vols. (completed by Lars-G. Hallander et al.) Stockholm Studies in English 34, 48. Stockholm: Almqvist & Wiksell, 1975–78.

Carnicelli, Thomas A., ed. *King Alfred's Version of St. Augustine's "Soliloquies."* Cambridge, Mass.: Harvard University Press, 1969.

Cockayne, Thomas Oswald, ed. "The Blooms of King Alfred." *The Shrine: A Collection of Occasional Papers on Dry Subjects.* London: 1864–70, 163–204.

Colgrave, Bertram (general editor). *The Paris Psalter (ms Bibliothèque Nationale Fonds Latin 8824).* Early English Manuscripts in Facsimile 8. Copenhagen: Rosenkilde & Bagger, 1958.

Dobbie, Elliott van Kirk. *The Anglo-Saxon Minor Poems.* The Anglo-Saxon Poetic Records 6. New York: Columbia University Press, 1942; reprint, 1968.

Endter, Wilhelm, ed. *König Alfreds des Grossen Bearbeitung der Soliloquien des Augustinus.* Bibliothek der angelsächsischen Prosa 11. Hamburg, 1922; reprint, Darmstadt: Wissenschaftliche Buchgesellschaft, 1964.

Hamilton, N. E. S. A., ed. *Willelmi Malmesbiriensis Monachi De Gestis Pontificum Anglorum Libri Quinque*. Rolls Series 52. London: 1870.

Hargrove, Henry L., ed. *King Alfred's Old English Version of St. Augustine's Soliloquies*. Yale Studies in English 13. New York: Henry Holt & Co., 1902.

————, trans. *King Alfred's Old English Version of St. Augustine's Soliloquies, turned into Modern English*. Yale Studies in English 22. New York: Henry Holt & Co., 1904.

Hecht, Hans, ed. *Bischof Wærferths von Worcester Übersetzung der Dialoge Gregors des Grossen*. 2 vols. Bibliothek der angelsächsischen Prosa 5. Leipzig, 1900–1907; reprint. 1 vol. Darmstadt: Wissenschaftliche Buchgesellschaft, 1965.

Hulme, William H., ed. " 'Blooms' von König Aelfred." *Englische Studien* 18 (1893):331–56.

Ker, N. R., ed. *The Pastoral Care: King Alfred's Translation of St. Gregory's Regula Pastoralis*. Early English Manuscripts in Facsimile 6. Copenhagen: Rosenkilde & Bagger, 1956.

Kotzor, Günter, ed. *Das altenglische Martyrologium*. Abhandlungen der bayerische Akademie der Wissenschaften, phil.-hist. Klasse 88. 2 vols. Munich: Bayerischen Akademie der Wissenschaften, 1981.

Krapp, George Philip. *The Paris Psalter and the Meters of Boethius*. The Anglo-Saxon Poetic Records 5. New York: Columbia University Press, 1932; reprint, 1970.

Liebermann, F., ed. *Die Gesetze der Angelsachsen*. 3 vols. Halle, 1903–16; reprint, Aalen: Scientia, 1960.

Miller, Thomas, ed. *The Old English Version of Bede's Ecclesiastical History of the English People*. Early English Text Society, Original Series 95, 96, 110, 111. London: Oxford University Press 1890–98; reprint, 1959–63.

Sedgefield, Walter J., ed. *King Alfred's Old English Version of Boethius, De Consolatione Philosophiae*. Oxford: Clarendon Press, 1899; reprint, Darmstadt: Wissenschaftliche Buchgesellschaft, 1968.

————. *King Alfred's Version of the Consolations of Boethius, done into Modern English*. Oxford: Clarendon Press, 1900.

Sisam, Celia, and Kenneth Sisam, eds., *The Salisbury Psalter*. Early English Text Society, Original Series 242. London: Oxford University Press, 1959; reprint, 1969.

Stevenson, William Henry, ed. *Asser's Life of King Alfred*. Oxford: Clarendon Press, 1904.

Stubbs, William, ed. *Willelmi Malmesbiriensis Monachi De Gestis Regum Anglorum Libri Quinque*. 2 vols. Rolls Series 90. London: 1887–89.

Sweet, Henry, ed. *King Alfred's West-Saxon Version of Gregory's Pastoral Care*. 2 vols. Early English Text Society, Original Series 45, 50. London: Oxford University Press 1871–72; reprint, 1958, with corrections by Neil R. Ker.

Turk, Milton Haight. *The Legal Code of Ælfred the Great.* Boston, 1893.

Whitelock, Dorothy. *English Historical Documents c. 500–1042.* 2d. ed. English Historical Documents 1. London: Eyre Methuen, 1979.

Wright, Cyril E., ed. *Bald's Leechbook: British Museum Royal ms 12 D.xvii.* Early English Manuscripts in Facsimile 5. Copenhagen: Rosenkilde & Bagger, 1955.

SECONDARY SOURCES

Bacquet, Paul. *La Structure de la phrase verbale à l'époque alfrédienne.* Paris: Les Belles Lettres, 1962. A detailed study of Old English syntax based on Alfred's works and other ninth-century texts.

Bately, Janet. "The Compilation of the Anglo-Saxon Chronicle, 60 B.C. to A.D. 890: Vocabulary as Evidence." *Proceedings of the British Academy* 64 (1980 for 1978):93–129. A study of lexical usage; argues that Alfred did not write the 890 Chronicle (the earliest version).

————. "King Alfred and the Old English Translation of Orosius." *Anglia* 88 (1970):433–60. A lexical comparison between Alfred's translations and the *Orosius;* argues that he did not write the latter.

————. "Lexical Evidence for the Authorship of the Prose Psalms in the Paris Psalter." *Anglo-Saxon England* 10 (1982):69–95. An excellent discussion of the use of lexical differences to determine authorship; argues that Alfred translated the first fifty psalms.

————. *The Literary Prose of King Alfred's Reign: Translation or Transformation?* London: University of London, 1980. Reprinted with *addenda et corrigenda* in the *Old English Newsletter,* ed. Paul E. Szarmach, Subsidia 10 (Binghamton, N.Y.: Center for Medieval and Early Renaissance Studies, 1984). A comparative analysis of Alfred's Boethius, the psalms, and the *Orosius;* argues that they "transform" as well as translate Latin.

Berkhout, Carl T. "Research on Early Old English Literary Prose, 1973–1982." In *Studies in Earlier Old English Prose,* edited by Paul E. Szarmach. Albany: State University of New York Press, 1986. An update of the Greenfield-Robinson bibliography listing many works concerning Alfred and ninth-century texts.

Bolton, Whitney F. "How Boethian is Alfred's *Boethius?*" In Szarmach, *Studies.* A comparison of Alfred's translation and its Latin source; argues that Alfred's is remote from Boethius's text in form and substance.

Borinski, Ludwig. *Der Stil König Alfreds: Eine Studie zur Psychologie der Rede.* Leipzig: Bernhard Tauchnitz, 1934. The only psychologically based study of word order and syntax of Old English prose; original, stimulating, and sadly neglected.

Bromwich, J. I'A. "Who Was the Translator of the Prose Portion of the Paris Psalter?" In *The Early Cultures of North-West Europe,* edited by Cyril Fox and Bruce Dickins, 289–303. Cambridge: Cambridge University Press, 1950. Tentative arguments favoring Alfred's authorship of this text.

Brooks, N. P. "England in the Ninth Century: the Crucible of Defeat." *Transactions of the Royal Historical Society,* 5th ser. 29 (1979):1–20. A gloomy view of ninth-century literary history.

Brown, William H., Jr. *A Syntax of King Alfred's "Pastoral Care."* The Hague: Mouton, 1970. A preliminary investigation of word order in this text; highly specialized.

Clement, Richard W. "The Production of the *Pastoral Care:* King Alfred and His Helpers." In Szarmach, *Studies.* An important examination of the interrelationships of the manuscripts of Alfred's translation of this text.

Davis, R. H. C. "Alfred the Great: Propaganda and Truth." *History* 56 (1971):169–82. A controversial argument about Alfred's attempts to manipulate historical writing to advance his political causes.

Duckett, Eleanor Shipley. *Alfred the Great: The King and His England.* Chicago: University of Chicago Press, 1956. Somewhat old-fashioned and admiring, but a readable, well-informed, and useful biography by a first-rate historian.

Fisher, D. J. V. *The Anglo-Saxon Age.* London: Longman, 1973. An excellent introductory study with a strong emphasis on political history, c. 400–1042.

Galbraith, V. H. "Who Wrote Asser's Life of Alfred?" *An Introduction to the Study of History.* London: C. A. Watts, 1964, 88–128. An exceptionally controversial attack on the authenticity of Asser's text.

Gatch, Milton McC. "King Alfred's Version of Augustine's *Soliloquia:* Some Suggestions on its Rationale and Unity." In Szarmach, *Studies.* The best analysis yet written of this difficult text and its Latin source.

Gibson, Margaret, ed. *Boethius: His Life, Thought and Influence.* Oxford: Basil Blackwell, 1981. A richly varied collection of essays examining all aspects of Boethius's writing.

Gneuss, Helmut. "A Preliminary List of Manuscripts Written or Owned in England up to 1100." *Anglo-Saxon England* 9 (1981):1–60. An invaluable beginning to a complete catalogue of manuscripts known to the Anglo-Saxons in England.

———— . "The Origin of Standard Old English and Æthelwold's School at Winchester." *Anglo-Saxon England* 1 (1972):63–83. A seminal work which argues for the development of a "standard" or literary language in the tenth century.

Greenfield, Stanley B. *A Critical History of Old English Literature.* New York: New York University Press, 1968. Soon to be updated, still an important standard survey of Old English poetry and prose.

Greenfield, Stanley B., and Fred C. Robinson, *A Bibliography of Publications on Old English Literature to the End of 1972.* Toronto: University of Toronto Press, 1980. An indispensable reference work, updated by Berkhout (see above).

Hinton, David. *Alfred's Kingdom: Wessex and the South. 800–1500.* London: Dent, 1977. A good analysis of political geography in Alfred's England.

Horgan, Dorothy M. "The Relationship between the OE Manuscripts of King Alfred's Translation of Gregory's *Pastoral Care.*" *Anglia* 91 (1973):153–69. A comparison of linguistic features of seven manuscripts of the text; includes a tentative stemma of the manuscripts.

Hunter-Blair, Peter. *An Introduction to Anglo-Saxon England,* 2d. ed. Cambridge: Cambridge University Press, 1976. A standard survey with a good bibliography.

Ker, N. R. *Catalogue of Manuscripts Containing Anglo-Saxon.* Oxford: Clarendon Press, 1957. A standard reference guide to Old English manuscripts; supplemented by the same author in *Anglo-Saxon England* 5 (1976):121–31.

Keynes, Simon, and Michael Lapidge. *Alfred the Great: Asser's "Life of King Alfred" and other Contemporary Sources.* New York: Penguin, 1983. An outstanding contribution to the scholarship: contains a fresh translation of the *Life* and parts of Alfred's translations and copious notes on historical and literary context.

Kirby, D. P. "Asser and His Life of King Alfred." *Studia Celtica* 6 (1971):12–35. A notorious attack on the value of Asser's *Life,* stimulating but to be regarded with skepticism.

———— . *The Making of Early England.* London: Batsford, 1967. A standard survey, especially rich in its discussion of social and cultural history.

Loyn, H. R. *Alfred the Great.* Oxford: Oxford University Press, 1967. A brief but useful overview.

———— . *Anglo-Saxon England and the Norman Conquest.* London: Longman, 1962. Social and economic history; authoritative, with an excellent bibliography.

Mapp, Alfred J., Jr. *The Golden Dragon: Alfred the Great and His Times.* LaSalle, Ill.: Open Court, 1974. A fictionalized biography of Alfred which vividly recreates a ninth-century world.

Metcalf, Allan A. *Poetic Diction in the Old English Meters of Boethius.* De Proprietatibus Litterarum, series practica, 50. The Hague and Paris: Mouton, 1973. A detailed investigation of the language of the text.

Morrish, Jennifer. "King Alfred's Letter as a Source on Learning in England." In Szarmach, *Studies.* A bracing and useful essay about ninth-century literary history, much broader than its title suggests.

O'Neill, Patrick P. "The Old English Introductions to the Prose Psalms of the Paris Psalter: Sources, Structure, and Composition." In *Eight Anglo-Saxon Studies,* edited by Joseph Wittig, 20–38. *Studies in Philology* 78. Chapel Hill, North Carolina, 1981. The first detailed investigation of the Introductions in the context of early medieval psalter study.

Otten, Kurt. *König Alfreds Boethius.* Studien zur englischen Philologie, N. F. 3. Tübingen: Max Niemeyer, 1964. A detailed comparison of the Old English text to the Latin source; a careful study of language, and the best book written on Alfred's *Consolation.*

Parkes, M. B. "The Palaeography of the Parker Manuscript of the *Chronicle,* Laws and Sedulius, and Historiography at Winchester in the Late Ninth Century." *Anglo-Saxon England* 5 (1976):149–71. An important survey of manuscripts and manuscript-production in Winchester during Alfred's reign and shortly thereafter.

Payne, F. Anne. *King Alfred and Boethius: An Analysis of the Old English Version of the Consolation of Philosophy.* Madison, Wis.: University of Wisconsin Press, 1968. A very modern argument about Alfred's translation, poorly documented and speculative.

Plummer, Charles. *The Life and Times of Alfred the Great.* Oxford: Clarendon Press, 1902. Victorian scholarship at its best; essential reading.

Potter, Simeon. "King Alfred's Last Preface." In *Philologica: The Malone Anniversary Studies,* edited by Thomas A. Kirby and Henry Bosley Woolf, 25–30. Baltimore: Johns Hopkins University Press, 1949. Argues, against strong evidence, that Alfred's Preface to the *Soliloquies* is complete.

Rand, E. K. *Founders of the Middle Ages.* Cambridge, Mass.: Harvard University Press, 1928; reprint, New York: Dover, 1957. An important look at several late Latin authors, including Boethius and Augustine, in an early medieval context.

Richards, Mary P. "The Manuscript Contexts of the Old English Laws: Tradition and Innovation." In Szarmach, *Studies.* A comprehensive discussion of the manuscripts of the laws.

Schütt, Marie. "The Literary Form of Asser's *Vita Alfredi.*" *English Historical Review* 62 (1957): 209–20. Places the text in the tradition of medieval hagiography and history.

Sisam, Kenneth. *Studies in the History of Old English Literature.* Oxford: Clarendon Press, 1953. A collection of wide-ranging, influential essays; includes an important chapter on the *Pastoral Care*.

Stenton, F. M. *Anglo-Saxon England*, 3d. ed. Oxford: Clarendon Press, 1971. The standard history of the period.

Stevenson, William Henry. "The Date of King Alfred's Death." *English Historical Review* 13 (1898):71–77. Establishes that Alfred died in 899 rather than 901.

Szarmach, Paul E. "The Meaning of Alfred's *Preface* to the *Pastoral Care*." *Mediaevalia* 6 (1982 for 1980):57–86. A close reading of the prefaces to the *Pastoral Care* and the *Soliloquies*.

————, ed. *Studies in Earlier Old English Prose*. Albany: State University of New York Press, 1986. An important collection of essays concerning Alfred's translations and other ninth-century texts.

————, and Bernard F. Huppé, eds. *The Old English Homily and Its Backgrounds*. Albany: State University of New York Press, 1978. An uneven but useful anthology of essays concerning later Old English prose.

Tinkler, John D. *Vocabulary and Syntax of the Old English Version in the Paris Psalter*. The Hague: Mouton, 1971. A study of the problematical linguistic and syntactical features of the text; includes comments on translation technique.

Wallace-Hadrill, J. M. *Early Germanic Kingship in England and on the Continent*. Oxford: Clarendon Press, 1971. Sets Anglo-Saxon kings in a continental perspective; many important observations about Alfred.

————. "The Franks and the English in the Ninth Century: Some Common Historical Interests." In *Early Medieval History*. New York: Barnes and Noble, 1975, 201–16. An important discussion of traditions shared by the Continent and Alfred's England.

Waterhouse, Ruth. "Tone in Alfred's Version of St. Augustine's *Soliloquies*." In Szarmach, *Studies*. The fullest examination of the literary features of Alfred's translation.

Whitelock, Dorothy. *From Bede to Alfred: Studies in Early Anglo-Saxon Literature and History*. London: Variorum Reprints, 1980. An important collection of previously published essays.

————. *History, Law, and Literature*. London: Variorum Reprints, 1981. Previously published essays, several concerning Anglo-Saxon.

————. "The Old English Bede." *Proceedings of the British Academy* 48 (1962):57–90. Examines the authorship of the translation of the *Ecclesiastical History*.

————. "The Prose of Alfred's Reign." In *Continuations and Beginnings: Studies in Old English Literature*, edited by E. G. Stanley, 67–103. London: Nelson, 1966. Still considered the best comprehensive survey of Alfred's prose; analyzes authorship and sources.

————— . "William of Malmesbury on the Works of King Alfred." In *Medieval Literature and Civilization: Studies in Memory of G. N. Garmonsway*, edited by D. A. Pearsall and R. A. Waldron, 78–93. London: Athlone, 1969. Examines the canon of Alfred's works as established by William.

Wittig, Joseph S. "King Alfred's *Boethius* and Its Latin Sources: A Reconsideration." *Anglo-Saxon England* 11 (1983 for 1982):157–98. The best and most recent study of the relationship of Alfred's *Consolation* to commentaries on Boethius.

Wülker, Richard P. *Grundriss zur Geschichte der angelsächsischen Litteratur*. Leipzig, 1885. A comprehensive survey including studies of several of Alfred's works.

Wrenn, C. L. *A Study of Old English Literature*. New York: W. W. Norton & Co., 1967. A general survey, a complement to Greenfield's *Critical History*.

Index

DATE DUE
